Keeping Your Kids Afloat When It Feels Like You're Sinking

Keeping Your Kids Afloat
When It Feels Like You're Sinking

CYNDI LAMB CURRY

SERVANT PUBLICATIONS
ANN ARBOR, MICHIGAN

Vine Books is an imprint of Servant Publications especially designed to serve evangelical Christians.

Servant Publications—Mission Statement
We are dedicated to publishing books that spread the gospel of Jesus Christ, help Christians to live in accordance with that gospel, promote renewal in the church, and bear witness to Christian unity.

Scripture verses, unless otherwise indicated, are from the Holy Bible, New International Version. Copyright 1973, 1978, 1984 by International Bible Society. Used by permission of Zondervan Publishing House. All rights reserved. Scripture verses marked THE MESSAGE are from The Message. Copyright by Eugene H. Peterson 1993, 1994, 1995. Used by permission of NavPress Publishing Group. Scripture verses marked LB are taken from The Living Bible copyright 1971. Used by permission of Tyndale House Publishers, Inc., Wheaton, Illinois 60189. All rights reserved.

All the stories in this book are true. Some names and identifying details have been changed to protect the privacy of those involved.

Published by Servant Publications
P.O. Box 8617
Ann Arbor, Michigan 48107
www.servantpub.com

Cover design: UDG/Designworks, Sisters, Oreg.

02 03 04 05 10 9 8 7 6 5 4 3 2 1

Printed in the United States of America
ISBN 1-56955-288-6

Library of Congress Cataloging-in-Publication Data
Curry, Cyndi Lamb, 1952-
   Keeping your kids afloat when it feels like you're sinking / Cyndi Lamb Curry.
         p. cm.
Includes bibliographical references.
   ISBN 1-56955-288-6 (perm. paper)
  1. Parenting. 2. Parent and child. 3. Parenting--Religious aspects.
4. Child rearing--Religious aspects. I. Title.
   HQ755.8 .C87 2002
   649'.1--dc21

                                                      2002009963

To Steve,
who modeled for all of us
how to stay afloat
in the deepest of waters,
and to our children,
Jeremy, Tate, and Katelyn,
who hung on to their life rafts ...
and to their faith.

Contents

1. You Can Get Through the Storm 9

Section One: Give Your Children Life Preservers

2. Be the Parent 17
3. Tell the Truth 21
4. Reassure Them 31
5. Let Them Grieve in Their Own Way 37
6. Listen Without Reacting 47
7. Be Present 53
8. Major on Majors 57
9. Keep Them Connected 63
10. Preserve Memories, Make New Traditions 73
11. Point Them to the Father 81
12. Get Help When You Need It 91

Section Two: Be an Anchor

13. You Are Your Children's Anchor 101
14. Anchor Yourself in Christ 107
15. Take Care of Yourself 113
16. Let Go of Anger and Resentment 119
17. Get a Support Network 127
18. Pray! 131
19. An Attitude of Gratitude 143
20. Letting Go 149
21. Redefine Yourself 155
22. Develop an Eternal Perspective 161

Epilogue 165
Notes 169
Bibliography 173

ONE

You Can Get Through the Storm

A renowned college coach had an unusual technique for training his swimmers. Instead of working with them in the pool, he drove them every afternoon to the local river, ordered them into the water and directed them to begin swimming upstream. Meanwhile, he sat on the riverbank in his folding chair, enjoying the scenery.

His swimmers struggled as the water rushed and tumbled past them. Despite their most determined efforts, they made little or no headway against the current. Worse than that, they soon lost ground as the river pushed them farther and farther downstream from their starting point. At the end of the workout, the coach would drive the school van along the river and pick up his exhausted athletes from their various stopping points.

Day after day he brought his load of frustrated swimmers to the river's edge and watched them plow into the swiftly flowing water. Finally, one young man dragged his trembling body out onto the rocky bank, walked over to the coach and proclaimed, "I quit!"

"Why?" asked the coach.

"Because I'm sick of this. We come out here every day and bust ourselves in this water while you sit around doing nothing. We're getting nowhere. This is impossible. We'll never be able to swim up this river, and I'm through trying."

"But I never intended for you to swim up the river," the older man replied.

"Then why in the world do you have us out here?"

The seasoned coach looked at his student. "Let me ask you something. At the end of our session yesterday, were you closer to your original starting point than you were on your first day out here?"

"Yes—but what does that mean?" returned the exasperated swimmer.

"That means you're making progress. Sometimes the best progress appears to be no progress at all. But if you can maintain your position against these rapids, think of what you can do in a placid pool. You're building stamina and strength and muscle out here. That's what I'm after."

All of us have times in our lives when we appear to be making little or no progress. Crises such as divorce, the death of a loved one, illness or disabilities are storms that threaten to drown us. During such times, all we can do is try to stay afloat. If your family is in such a place, this book is for you.

Although each family's situation is unique, I have an idea what you're going through. Believe me when I tell you: *Whatever is going on, you can get through this—and so can your kids.*

My Family's Story

At the time my story begins, my husband, our two boys and I were living in a small subdivision outside Oklahoma City. Several miles of undeveloped pasture surrounded the housing development, so we had the best of both worlds—a country feel within a neighborhood.

Steve, thirty-eight years old, was an account executive for our state's largest news/talk radio station. He sold time to companies to advertise on the station's airwaves, and it was a career made for him. He loved to write and produce commercials. He had excellent people skills and he was a creative whirlwind. And besides being a pacesetter in his industry, he was able to use his position as a platform for ministry.

On the last Sunday of 1991, one of our sons awoke with a fever. Because both Steve and I had children's church responsibilities, he suggested I stay home and get a little extra rest while he carried out our duties. Right before he left, he kissed me on the cheek and then on my tummy. I was pregnant, and he was so excited about having a daughter.

A little later I waddled out to the kitchen to begin lunch preparations. Before long the phone rang. I was stunned to learn that a drunk driver had hit Steve's car. My husband was in critical condition at the hospital.

Unexpectedly Steve survived, but a brain injury left him in a coma. Just seven weeks after his accident, I went into the same hospital where he lay unconscious and gave birth to our third child, a daughter.

Steve remained in a coma for five months and in the hospital for another year and a half. When he finally began to emerge from the coma, he could only move his right arm and hand, and he had difficulty speaking. The injury to his brain left him with short-term memory loss and other cognitive impairments. And when he finally returned home, twenty-three months after the accident, he couldn't walk, drive or work. He had to have someone get him out of bed in the morning and put him into bed at night. He couldn't even get himself to the bathroom.

Everything in my life changed as I struggled to be the wife he needed and the mom my kids required. Adjustment was slow and difficult, but five-and-a-half years after the accident, we had finally adapted to Steve's situation.

We were within weeks of moving into a newly built, handicapped-accessible home when Steve began to have some alarming symptoms. He seemed more lethargic during the day and increasingly restless at night. Amidst his protests that he was "just fine," I took him to the doctor. Within hours of his appointment, he was diagnosed with advanced leukemia. Six days later he was dead.

Another storm engulfed us. Sometimes I didn't think we would make it, but with God's help and the support of caring family and friends, we did. We were blessed to be part of a faith community that blew up the life rafts and headed out to the deep waters with us. The love and support we received from our church family and natural family made a tremendous difference, although God had to teach me that it was okay to ask for and accept help.

In the end, my relationship with the Father proved to be my strongest support. I had developed this crazy notion that God really loved me—and my children and Steve. In the darkest nights of my soul, when I had no idea how we were going to make it, terrified of what might lie ahead, God was there.

I wrote this book to give you hope as you go through your own dark place ... hope that you will come out on the other side of it. I also wanted to give you some insight and practical advice to help you and your family navigate the rocky waters around you. In Section One you'll find some life-preserving principles that will help you understand what your children most need from you during difficult times. Section Two will help you be the anchor your kids need you to be while the storms of life threaten your family's well-being.

I pray that some of what I learned in the midst of my storm will help you keep your kids afloat until the turmoil in your life subsides. In times of crisis, sometimes keeping afloat is the only kind of progress we can make.

Section One

Give Your Children Life Preservers

TWO

Be the Parent

Our daughter, Katelyn, who was born seven weeks after Steve's accident, had no awareness that her family's life was in such turmoil. Each morning I would hear her cooing in her crib as she awakened. She greeted me with squeals of delight as I dragged my tired body and heavy heart into the nursery. Her two brothers would join us and we'd start our day off with a joy-fest around her bed.

Katelyn's sweet disposition and innocence brought a much-needed lightness to our hearts and home. I had not anticipated how cheerful she would be. She gave me a reason to get up and go on. And while I might have been able to fool myself that our two boys, ages ten and six, could manage without so much of me, I could not deny that a newborn needed her mother. Having a baby in the house helped me see that my sons needed me as well.

Your children need you—now more than ever. When life is difficult and you are tempted to check out, don't succumb. You are the only parent(s) your children have. When families experience tragedy and crisis, we parents are called upon to perform extraordinary tasks. Not only do we have to deal with our own feelings of loss, but we also have to continue to parent our children in a healthy way. This is a gargantuan feat. And yet, it's possible.

Jackie's girls lost their dad to mental illness. "Parenting two teenagers alone is challenging," Jackie says, "but I made a conscious choice to do the right thing, to put their needs ahead of mine. A parent has to be willing to sacrifice, willing to see the long-term end result. It's not always easy to do, but I have tried."

Research backs up Jackie's instincts:

> Ironically when adults get down to the business of parenting and focus on children's needs, it actually makes this transition smoother. It gets you outside yourself—forces you to rise to a higher purpose.... Keeping your mind on what your children need not only mitigates the harmful effects ... on them, it also helps to diffuse your own feelings of loss and self-pity.[1]

When her husband, Fred, died in an accident while coming home from a mission trip, Ami made a conscious decision not to wallow in self-pity. "I had other widows coming up to me and saying, 'Oh, honey, you'll never get over it,'" she says. "I was horrified. I thought, *I can't do that to myself or my three children.*"

Your kids need you to retain your role as the parent. They need you to provide not only for their physical needs—food, clothing and shelter—they also need you to meet their emotional needs. When their world has been turned upside down by loss, whether through death, divorce or illness, children require stability and love more than anything else.

Those who have lost a spouse can be tempted to allow one of their kids to become the parent. We call this the *parentification* of children. To avoid this:

- **Do not let your child become your emotional support.**

  When you are in pain, you may be tempted to turn to your child for emotional support. DON'T. While it is okay for children to see you sad, it is not okay to lean on them. Do not count on children to fill the gap in your life that the loss has left. Do not expect them to alleviate your loneliness.

- **Do not confide in your children.**

  Without another adult in the house it is easy to unload on your children. Do not talk to your kids about your money problems, your fears, your anger with your ex, your relationships. And don't let them overhear you discuss these issues, either.

- **Do not turn your house into a child-centered home.**

  As much as possible, keep family rules the same after a crisis as before. When we as parents are in pain, it's tempting to abdicate our role as the leader of the home. When we do, we let the child set the emotional stage for the family. Instead, we must take charge and establish clear boundaries and rules. Do not tolerate bad behavior or let your kids off the hook when they act irresponsibly or don't do their household chores. If you are plagued with guilt for something you did— such as divorcing your spouse—don't try to make it up to your kids by going easy on them or overindulging them with gifts and privileges. While this may seem easier at the time, in the long run overindulgence is harmful to children.

- **Don't put too much responsibility on the shoulders of children.**

  This is the opposite of not requiring enough. Be careful not to expect children to take on too many household chores such as cooking and looking after younger siblings. Remember they are still children. Encourage them to resume their normal activities.

You will likely feel overwhelmed for a while. That's normal. The feeling will eventually pass. In the meantime, however, remind yourself often that you have a responsibility to parent your children. You cannot crawl into a hole. You cannot lock yourself in a box. You cannot fly away to a deserted island. But you can run to God and allow him to guide you as you become the best parent you can be.

THREE

Tell the Truth

A nd what are my husband's chances?" I asked, not really wanting to hear the answer.

"I'd say only fair," Dr. Bryan responded. "If he makes it through the night, then we're out of the woods. All we can do now is wait."

Only fair. I caught those words as if they were an overweight package. I held them, feeling I might collapse under their load at any moment. *This can't be happening. Not to my Steve. Not to this dynamic, energetic ball of life.* Like a robot, I signed permission forms for the surgeon to perform a tracheotomy on my thirty-eight-year-old husband, a procedure he assured me was necessary for Steve to have even a fighting chance to survive.

Once the surgery was completed, I needed to call our sons and give them an update. They knew their dad had been in a car accident, but little else. I struggled with what to tell them. Should I repeat the doctor's prediction that Steve had only a "fair" chance to make it through the night? Or should I wait until the morning when I knew more? I decided that my sons were too young to handle the news that their dad might die, but I did tell them that he had been in a car wreck and was badly hurt and unconscious.

If you are dealing with a family crisis, you have faced a similar dilemma: how much should you tell your children? The amount of information you give your child will vary according to the child's age, temperament and emotional state. In general, children will respond best if you tell them what is happening, keep them updated with appropriate information, use language they understand and let them know what to expect in the future.

Tell Your Children What Is Happening

Many parents worry about telling children too much, but most err by not telling enough. Wyndi and Bryan had avoided talking to their eight-year-old daughter about a tumor that had started to grow in Wyndi's neck. They wanted to avoid alarming Hannah while they awaited test results. Yet Hannah could see the growth and was left to her own devices to figure it out. Fortunately, a wise counselor intervened and encouraged them to talk with her about the growth.

"Hannah," Wyndi began, "maybe you've noticed Mommy seems a little preoccupied ..."

"What's that mean?" Hannah asked.

"It means that I've been acting like I'm thinking about something else and not really focused on you or Daddy or what is going on here and now."

"I don't know," Hannah replied.

"Well, I just wanted to let you know what's going on with me. I have a growth in my neck that I've been to see the doctor about."

"What's a growth?"

"It's kind of like a round ball of tissue under my skin that is not usually there. We're not sure what made it grow or what we need to do about it. The doctor is checking on it. When he knows more about what kind of tissue it is, he will know how we should treat it. I just thought I should let you know why I may seem a little distracted right now. As soon as I know more, I'll tell you. Do you have any questions?"

"No," was all Hannah said, but Wyndi and Bryan felt relieved and sensed that Hannah did also.

Children, even very young children, sense when something is wrong. Many times, in our desire to protect them, we lie or avoid talking to our kids at all. This is far more harmful than helpful. When adults hide information from them, children feel excluded and are likely to imagine what is wrong—and that can often be worse than reality.

When author Gary Neuman was a boy, his parents told him not to hang his body out the car window, but they didn't tell him why. Gary soon figured it out for himself after watching *The Flintstones* and seeing what happened when the cartoon characters hung out their automobile window: the car tipped over. Now he understood!

We may laugh, but when children don't have an explanation for the events in their lives, they are "driven to explain the world to themselves.... Children embrace beliefs and harbor fears that we cannot imagine."[1]

Keep Your Children Updated

It's not enough to talk to your children one time about what is happening in your home. You need to keep a running dialogue going, repeating what you have already told them and giving them new information as it develops.

This is not always easy. We may sense our children are not anxious to hear any more "bad news." But while they may not want to hear it, they need to hear it, and they need to hear it from their parents.

Don't feel you have to sit down every evening for a formal news update. In fact, it's better if you can talk to your children as you go about your day. Sometimes it's easier to discuss difficult subjects "shoulder-to-shoulder" rather than face-to-face. Take advantage of drive time in the car, or as you clean up after a meal or throw a ball in the backyard with your child.

One of the most common reactions to loss for all children is decreased concentration. Therefore, continue to give information to your children over and over until you are sure they remember and understand.

Keep Your Communication Appropriate

While children need to know the truth about what has happened— for instance, that Mom and Dad are getting a divorce—they may not need to know that Mom is divorcing Dad because of his perpetual unfaithfulness. And what you tell a four-year-old will be different from what you tell a fourteen-year-old. Answer their questions honestly while avoiding unnecessary details.

As much as possible, relay facts accurately without dumping your adult concerns on your kids. For instance, you may tell your children that you need to be extra careful with money so you are going to start borrowing videos from the library instead of renting them, playing more games at home and eating out less. But you do not need to share with them all your financial anxieties.

To alleviate their fears, for instance, you might assure them (if it's true): "We will stay in this house, and we will have plenty to eat." But don't use specific dollar amounts. To tell a child you only have one hundred dollars left until the next paycheck can be confusing, since one hundred dollars to most children is a lot of money.

You will also want to shield your children from emotions that will wound them. It's okay for kids to see you sad, hurt or crying. It is not good for them to see you out of control with fear and rage. You don't have to pretend things are fine, but you also don't have to scream, "Your father is a jerk and I can't believe he's doing this to us."

Besides making sure that what you tell your children is appropriate, also guard what they hear you tell others. Children have remarkable hearing when it comes to adult conversations. Even when we think children are preoccupied with play or out of earshot, we can be fooled. Be diligent in protecting your children from adult discussions, especially when it involves conflict between you and their other parent.

Use Language Your Children Understand

When talking with children about what has happened or is happening, use language they can understand.

When talking about death. Using words that children can understand is particularly important when telling them that someone they love has died. Don't say, "Mommy has gone to sleep"—this can create a fear of sleeping in children. And don't tell them, "God was lonely and took your dad. He needed another angel in heaven." What does that communicate to children about God? Such a comment raises far more questions than it answers.

Simply say that the person has died. If the child doesn't understand what death is, you can say, "When someone dies, their body doesn't work anymore—it cannot move, it does not feel or think. Everything in the body stops working. The eyes can't see, the heart quits beating, the person can no longer breathe." Ask your child if she understands or if she has any questions. She may also need to know that death is irreversible—unlike some cartoon characters she sees on TV who die and come back to life.

We can offer our children hope by telling them about God's gift of heaven and a new body. We can teach them that in heaven there will no more pain, crying or death. "He will wipe every tear from their eyes. There will be no more death or mourning or crying or pain, for the old order of things has passed away" (Rev 21:4). We can comfort our children with the truth that Christians will see each other again one day.

When talking about suicide or murder. While talking to children about all kinds of death is difficult, nothing is harder than addressing suicide or murder. Many adults are tempted to hide suicide as the cause of death, hoping the child will not find out. When they do, children are sometimes left feeling somehow responsible for the death because no one wanted to tell them.

Since most suicides are related to clinical depression, you might say something like this: "Sometimes people's brains get sick and stop working right. We call that clinical depression. People with this disease are really, really, really sad about everything most of the time—not just a little sad, like all of us are some days." You may then want to explain some of the symptoms of clinical depression, such as weight loss or gain, low energy, isolation, sleeping changes.

You can also let a child know that there is medicine for this disease, but sometimes the brain is too sick for it to help, or sometimes people stop taking their medicine. "Then that person's brain *might* tell her to make her body stop working. When someone chooses to make their own body stop working, we call it suicide."[2] Then you can tell the child in simple and brief terms how his loved one died. Let your child know she can come to you as often as she wants to talk more or ask further questions.

When talking to a child about murder, it's best to begin with a gentle assertion: "Sometimes people do bad things and it hurts people, even people we love." Then give a brief description of what happened. "A man shot Daddy in his chest, his heart stopped working and he died." Eventually, families that have experienced a suicide or homicide often want more details. It's important to be honest while matching your answers to the child's ability to understand and cope with the information.

When talking about divorce. Research indicates that having an "explanation for the divorce that [a child] can understand is one of the best predictors of child adjustment after divorce,"[3] yet up to 80 percent of children are not given an explanation for their parents' parting.

Elizabeth's three children were seven, five and six months old when her husband left her for another woman. Talking about their separation and divorce with her kids has been one challenge she has faced repeatedly the last few years. Her five-year-old began with very literal questions: "Mom, why didn't you stand in the doorway and not let Dad go?" She had to explain to Jake that you can't make an adult stay when he doesn't want to.

Elizabeth put off giving her kids a reason for the divorce, unsure of how to answer. After hearing from her family counselor that the best response was to tell the truth on the child's level, she told them, "Your dad said he didn't love me anymore."

"Well, why?" Jake countered.

"If a mom or a dad is not careful, they can allow themselves to fall in love with someone else. This isn't what God wants in a marriage; he wants us to love only each other, but sometimes it happens."

Pondering that, Jake then asked, "Did Dad make a promise to you?"

She said, "Yes, that is what you do when you get married."

"Then why did he leave anyways?" he wondered.

"I had to tell him that his dad broke his promise to me," Elizabeth says, "and that was hard."

Like Elizabeth, you need to be truthful yet appropriate in your explanation. Instead of saying, "Daddy and I are getting a divorce because he has a girlfriend," she told Jake, "Daddy and I are getting a divorce because he says he doesn't love me anymore."

Let Your Children Know What To Expect in the Future

If a loved one is ill and dying, you can help to prepare a child by laying out the probable steps the illness will follow. You don't have to be graphic, but you can tell the child that the person may get weaker, not be able to do as many things as he normally could, or that he may need to go to the hospital. If and when death seems probable, you should tell your child.

In the case of divorce, children need to know what to expect. They will want to know how the divorce will affect them. Where will they live? Where will they go to school? When will they see their non-custodial parent? Do your best to anticipate all the changes that will affect them.

If your child has lost a parent suddenly, keep in mind that he may learn from the loss that relationships aren't forever. The loss of a parent can affect a child's ability to commit in future relationships. It may leave the child living life "waiting for the other shoe to drop." Watch for these symptoms in your child, and as he matures, talk about potential consequences. Encourage your child to talk about his feelings. Most of all, offer many reassurances of your love and care.

Deciding what and how much to tell children can be a tough call. You will do your children a favor by telling them the truth, repeatedly. Keeping them abreast of the family situation is one way to keep them afloat.

FOUR

Reassure Them

Jackie did not initiate a separation from her husband without lots of thoughtful consideration. But as Frank's progressive mental deterioration caused her concern for the family's safety, she devised a plan to move herself and the two girls out of their house and to her parents' home to live temporarily.

Just when she was ready to carry out the plan, Jackie's eight-year-old daughter, Amanda, broke her arm. Instead of taking her back home from the hospital, Jackie moved her into her grandparents' house. Jackie and her other daughter soon followed.

Years later, Amanda offhandedly remarked to her mom that if she hadn't broken her arm and needed extra help, the three of them might not have left their dad. All those years, Amanda had blamed herself for her parents' breakup!

Kids who are dealing with a family crisis not only need to know the truth about the situation, they also need your constant reassurance. In particular, they need to hear, "What happened is not your fault. You did not cause this, and you cannot fix it." And just as important: "I love you very much and will be here for you."

Assure Them: "This Is Not Your Fault"
Child development experts tell us that children often blame themselves when something bad happens at home or to a parent. They

believe that their thoughts or actions brought about the problem or crisis. They need to be told again and again that what happened is not their fault and that they can't fix it.

Abused or abandoned children may feel even more strongly that they are at fault. They think, *I must have done something very bad for my parent to do this to me.* If a parents' death is the result of a homicide, suicide or an accident, children may believe they could have prevented the death if only they had been there. They may wonder if they could have intervened by delaying the parent or apologizing for something they had done.

I'm grateful that a few days after my husband was hit by a drunk driver, a wise friend advised me to talk with my sons and assure them that their father's accident had nothing to do with them. A week after the accident, I drove through a local drive-in, ordered the three of us drinks, and then turned onto a busy thoroughfare.

"I want to ask you guys something," I began.

"Ask away," Jeremy replied easily.

"Well ... I want you to know that all children get mad at their parents. And they may wish ... at times ... that their parents would just go away or get sick or drop dead. I just wanted you to know that if you've ever felt that way or wished something like that, it has nothing to do with what has happened to your father. Your thoughts and wishes do not have that kind of power."

There. I'd said it. But did they understand? I thought I should find out.

"So ... have you ever felt that way or wished something like that with your dad?" I asked.

Silence.

In the dark from the other side of the car came Jeremy's reply:

"No, Mom, I've never felt that way toward Dad." Sip, sip. "But I have felt that way toward you."

"Oh ..." was all I could manage. I had tried to think of all their possible responses. This one had not occurred to me. I didn't know whether to laugh or cry so I just choked on my crushed ice.

I now look back on that exchange with a smile and a sense of satisfaction. At least for that moment all minds were clear!

Reassure Them: "I Love You and Will Be Here for You"

When I had to tell our eleven-year-old son, Tate, about Steve's leukemia, Tate's first question was, "Is Daddy going to die?" I told him I didn't know, but that it was very serious. His second question startled me: "Well, if he does, are you going to get remarried?"

I staggered around that one for a while, telling Tate that was the last thing on my mind right now. He insisted I address his question, refusing to drop it. Finally he said to me, "Well, you know what happened to Josh."

Suddenly the reason for his urgency became clear. Josh was a classmate whose mother had divorced Josh's father, remarried a man who "did not like her children," and moved thirteen hundred miles away, leaving Josh and his sister to be raised by their grandparents. Tate was really asking me, "What's going to happen to me if Daddy dies and you remarry?"

I reassured him that I would keep him and his brother and sister with me until they grew up and moved away from home. This satisfied him for a while, but I found that I needed to repeat it over and over again as the fear kept popping up.

All children need their parents' love and protection, but children who have experienced loss and tragedy have an even greater need. They have lost their innocence; they know firsthand that life can be hard and that things don't last. Now more than ever, your kids need to hear you say, "I love you and I will be here for you." You cannot say these words too often.

- Let them be the first words you say to your child in the morning and the last you say at night.
- Look your child in the eye and say them when he or she leaves for school or work or practice.
- Throughout the day say "I love you" to your child for no particular reason at all.
- Write a love note and stick it on the mirror, or in your son's lunch bag, or on your daughter's pillow.

"What If Something Happens to You?"
Sixty-two percent of children who lose a parent to death worry that the surviving parent will also die.[1] One ten-year-old who lost his father was so worried about his mother also dying that he would go into her bedroom late at night to make sure she was still breathing.[2] If your child asks, "But what if something happens to you?" tell him or her, "*Someone* will be here for you." Be prepared to give more information if they ask for it.

To do this you need to have a back-up plan in case something *should* happen to you. Begin to pray and ask God for direction. Talk to family members or friends. Make out a will. This is not something most of us enjoy doing, but it is a needed step in parenting your children.

Remember, kids need to know what to expect in the future. If your kids are concerned about what will happen to them if something happens to you, tell them who will take care of them should you become unable to do so. Give them as much concrete information as you can. Along with your continual pledge that you will always love them and be there for them, these concrete details will help ease their anxiety.

Divorce also raises anxiety about further loss or complete abandonment. "Children need a considerable amount of parental care to offset these terrible fears. They need to be reassured that you love them and they won't be left like you are leaving each other."[3]

After his divorce, Don made a conscious effort to keep communication lines open with his two sons, who were living with their mother. "I deliberately gave lots of hugs and kisses, lots of touch—even when they thought they were too big," he says.

Be Sure You Don't Pull Away

Sometimes, just when children need them the most, parents unconsciously pull away from their children—often because they feel the need to protect themselves from further pain.

My friend Elizabeth struggled with this when her husband walked out on her and her three young children. "At times I have pushed my kids away because I was so afraid of rejection again and so absorbed in my own hurt," she says. "God graciously brought this to my attention, and I have tried to hug when I don't feel like it and compliment when I am too busy and stop and listen when I am preoccupied."

One mother noticed that on the weekends when she didn't have custody of her children, she filled her time with a flurry of activity to deaden the pain. When the girls returned home on Sunday evenings, she couldn't slow down and reconnect with them. It was hard, but she had to make changes in her behavior so that she was ready to connect emotionally with her kids when they returned home.

Another mother said she didn't realize that she'd pulled away until one day she saw the pain in her son's eyes when he looked at her. She asked him if he'd like a hug, and he dove toward her and buried his head in her lap and cried.

Most children will not be able to tell you they feel that you are pulling away from them. But if you sense there is a distance or coolness in a formerly warm relationship, if your family members seem to be living *alone* under the same roof, if there are few shared moments, perhaps you need to step back and examine if you are the cause.

I have taught my daughter to tell me when she needs a hug. I have told her to "just tell me" with her words instead of pouting or acting forlorn and hoping I will notice. Sometimes when she tells me, "Mom, I want a hug," it opens us to conversation. Other times, we simply share a moment of closeness before we each go on about our lives.

As parents, we need to reverse any tendencies to hold our children at arm's length. We must make a conscious effort to connect with them—by talking, eating meals around the table (rather than in front of the TV), engaging in activities we all enjoy and always reassuring them of our love and commitment.

We must tell our children in our words, our hugs and our presence that we will continue to be in their lives to care for them. We can't do this too much!

FIVE

Let Them Grieve in Their Own Way

In the weeks following Steve's accident, our home teemed with visitors, flowers and food. Ten-year-old Jeremy's eyes lit up with each chocolate Bundt cake and plate of homemade cookies that entered the door. As I made room for new deliveries on the counter, he said to me, "Not to be rude, Mom, but it isn't so bad having Dad in the hospital when you get all these goodies."

At first I wanted to gasp in horror and set him straight. Then I realized he did not understand that his father was in serious condition—so serious, in fact, that he could die. Jeremy's words simply reflected who he was: a little boy who had never before encountered tragedy and who loved sweets and had never seen such an array of confectioneries in his life. In his mind, Dad would soon be better and back home. Meanwhile, *bon appétit!*

Children, because of their limited experience and knowledge, cannot see the world the way adults do. They may not know what is appropriate to do or say in times of crisis. One of the life supports we parents can offer our kids is to allow them to grieve in their own way.

Kids Often Express Their Grief in Ways Other Than Words

Counselors at the Kids' Place, a support group center for grieving children and their families in Oklahoma City, say that one of the biggest mistakes parents can make is to assume that their children are not experiencing any sense of loss. Parents make this judgment because the child doesn't cry or appear sad. But bursts of grief come in the middle of everyday life for children, as they do for adults, and we may not always be aware of them.

Many adolescents are not comfortable with showing emotion. Most are concerned about their image, what others think of them, and they do not want to appear different. They may harbor fears of "losing it" emotionally and not being able to regain control. For this reason, they may feel a torrent of emotions but appear to "have it all together."

Don't be fooled. If your child has suffered loss, he or she needs to grieve the loss in an understanding and supportive environment.

A child's stage of development will affect the way he or she grieves. In general, young children express their feelings of grief through play or art. After my father-in-law died, three-year-old Jeremy called me back to his room. With eyes closed, he lay still and stiff on his bed.

"What are you doing?" I asked.

"I'm Grandpa in a box," he replied, only moving his lips.

Jeremy had felt the impact of his grandfather's death on an emotional level, but without the cognitive ability to articulate his feelings, he reenacted his grandfather's funeral.

Parents can help young kids express their sadness by encouraging them to draw and by letting them play. To do this, have art supplies readily available. Ask your preschooler to draw a picture of your family now and to tell you about it. Use the picture as a springboard for discussing how he or she feels.

Parents can also help grieving kids by encouraging physical activity. Outdoor play is far more beneficial for them than sitting in front of television or computer screens. Encourage children to get outside and ride bikes, play basketball or roller blade. Do activities with them if possible: dig in the garden, walk the dog. Working or playing with your children serves as great family time as well as wonderful therapy.

Older kids, too, may benefit from physical activity—particularly boys. The day after his dad's death, sixteen-year-old Jeremy hopped on the riding lawnmower and mowed two overgrown acres. As an active teenage boy, he needed to do something physical rather than sit inside the house answering doorbells and handling phone calls. Mowing the lawn was therapeutic for Jeremy.

Later that summer, Jeremy spent lots of time with friends golfing and hanging out. He told me he felt guilty having so much fun right after his dad died, but I tried to help him understand that keeping busy is often a way adolescents deal with grief—that his response was normal and that it was okay.

Children Grieve in Spurts

Children don't grieve on an even, predictable plane. God designed them with an innate ability to judge how much pain they can handle at one time. They may initially respond to loss with sadness, but then run outside and play as if nothing had happened. They may take their grief down from the shelf, deal with it for a time, and then put it away until later.

This was certainly true of both our boys after Steve's accident. On one level they acted as if life were still the same—they went to school, participated in sports, played outside with neighbors in the afternoon. Many nights the evening meal seemed like any other evening when their dad might have worked late. We would talk about Jeremy's homework or how many girls chased Tate on the kindergarten playground that day. At other times, Steve's empty chair would trigger the boys' grief. On those nights, meals became a combat zone as the boys picked at one another while picking at their food. While there had always been plenty of sibling squabbles, after the accident they seemed nastier and more intense.

Bedtime, too, could trigger their grief because it was a time that Steve had often played his guitar and sung the boys to sleep. Even though Tate and Jeremy shared a bedroom upstairs and had each other for company, they had trouble falling asleep. In order to give them peace of mind and help them feel safer, I moved sleeping bags into my room on the floor next to my bed. I felt comforted by this as well.

Sometimes, after a rather uneventful day, I would lie in the bedroom with my sons and we would talk. In the dark and quiet room, one of them might start to cry. Then all of us would cry. Then we would pray. And sometimes we cried some more. The next morning they got up, went to school and played with their buddies in the afternoon. The previous night's dip into grief was over and life seemed "normal" again.

Children Often Grieve Through Explosive Emotions

When children express their grief, it may be in brief but intensive episodes of rage. Feelings of anger, blame, resentment and jealousy may surface. This is particularly true with boys, who often express their pain through anger because they think that anger shows strength. As a result, they may yell or stomp around or hit things.

One Saturday morning about six months after Steve's wreck, I heard a repetitive thumping outside and went to investigate. Without him seeing me, I watched Jeremy pick up rocks and slam them against the house. With each blow to the brick wall he yelled, "I hate my life." Jeremy's life had been horribly disrupted and though he didn't have the words to express his pain, with each rock he threw he was acting it out.

Initially I thought my son had really lost it. Then I realized he had found a non-destructive way to grieve.

While we shouldn't scold kids for their feelings, if they are acting out in negative ways—hitting, running or being overly aggressive, for instance—we need to guide them to find non-aggressive ways to release their emotions. For instance, you might buy a punching bag or pillow and direct your son to express his feelings by hitting it as much as he needs to for release. When your daughter starts acting out aggressively at home, tell her to shut the door and scream and yell at the bag or pillow.

If your child is acting aggressively in public, you may have to intervene. For example, one Sunday after church our family went out for pizza with friends. As we waited in line to order, Jeremy looked in his billfold and discovered ten dollars missing, money he had planned to use playing video games. He became so angry that he threw his wallet across the restaurant, where it whizzed past the heads of people waiting in line and landed next to the salad bar. Thankfully, it didn't hit anyone.

I took him aside and told him how inappropriate his behavior was. I said to him, "Jeremy, I know you are hurting. I know your life is hard right now, but that is no excuse for acting like this." He apologized and then asked if he could borrow some money. I said I would have been happy to earlier, but since he had acted out by throwing his billfold, I was not going to loan him any money. He was very angry with me and sat for the rest of the time alone, smoldering. I was pretty miserable too, but I felt as if I had to draw a line. The way he had chosen to express his anger was not okay.

Some Children May Temporarily Regress

All of us cling to the familiar when times are stressful. Children are no different. Grieving children may revert to earlier behaviors for a while. A younger child may want to return to using a pacifier or may cling to a special blanket or a favorite stuffed animal. Some children may have sleep disturbances or wet the bed.

Even adolescents can regress. Ellen noticed this in her fifteen-year-old daughter when her father was in critical condition after a car accident. His life hung in the balance. Without even realizing it, Christy began calling her parents Mommy and Daddy.

If your children begin to show signs of regression, don't be alarmed. Most of all, don't be critical of them. Usually these problems are short-term. You can help by giving additional hugs and by reassuring your children of your love and care.

Children Often Delay Their Grief

Grief experts tell us that children tend to delay their grieving process six to nine months until they are sure the surviving parent is coping. They seem to intrinsically know a parent may not be able to handle too much at one time. What a gift God has given us in this internal timing.

I was eating out with Jeremy several months after his dad's wreck. The restaurant was filled with families that all seemed exuberantly happy. It made me miss our old life. I asked Jeremy if he wished he were a part of one of these families. "Nope," he said matter-of-factly. "I'll just wait for my dad to come home."

I realized that Jeremy had not yet made any mental adjustment that his dad might not ever come home in the way he was expecting. But he did several months later. Jeremy came dripping down the hall following a shower; he was right up to me before I could tell he was crying.

"I just realized, Mom," he said between sobs, "that even if my dad does come back home and even if he is ever able to wrestle with me again, I may be so old that I won't even care about wrestling anymore. My dad is missing the rest of my childhood."

It was a hard but necessary transition that Jeremy had not been able to accept immediately.

This need for mental adjustment is not limited to homes where the crisis is illness or death. Most children in a divorced home harbor wishes for a reconciliation of their family. It is crucial for parents who know the divorce is final to be definitive about this with their children. When children fantasize about their parents reuniting, it keeps them from processing the change and moving on. Sometimes parents are unaware of the intensity of their children's fantasies.

Each of us needs to be allowed to process loss and grief at our own pace, including our kids. If, as parents, we can maintain an open and loving home where we allow sorrow and grief on a child's own terms, our kids will work out their grief. If, on the other hand, you insist that your child process his or her grief in a certain way and time, you may harm your child or your relationship with that child.

Children Revisit Loss

When children lose parents, they will continue to process their grief throughout their lives. As they reach the next developmental level, they will reprocess their loss through their new knowledge and understanding. Katelyn was five when Steve died. She fell asleep at the funeral. But when she was nine, she began to ask more questions about him, take items that had belonged to him to her room and keep his picture on her nightstand. Four years after his death, Katelyn realized more completely what it meant that her father had died and was not coming back. She was different than many of her friends, and her loss had impacted and continued to impact her day-to-day life. She had become more aware of what she was missing.

Children will also reprocess their grief at major milestones: significant birthdays, graduations, when they marry, when they have children of their own, when a parent remarries after death or divorce. When one of my sons attended his first church youth retreat, he came home enthusiastic about the weekend. After he described the music and speaker and the fun they'd had, he got quiet.

"Where did you just go?" I asked gently.

"Oh, I'm just thinking about how Don and Mike and Gary [dads who were sponsors] were in on all the pranks. And just realizing that if my dad would have been there, he would have been right in the middle of all that." He was right. Jeremy was reprocessing the loss of his dad at a significant moment in his life.

You can help your children by talking with them about grief and alerting them to this normal tendency. This will reduce their surprise and help them understand what they are feeling and why.

As your kids get older, you can encourage them to articulate their feelings and to cry if they feel like it. Don't try to talk them out of their sadness. Instead, accept how they feel, help them grieve appropriately, and encourage them to feel their sadness rather than "stuff" their feelings. This isn't easy, but in the long run it is far better for your kids.

If you want to help your children stay afloat when life threatens to drown them, let them grieve in their own way. Don't expect them to be miniature adults. Give them permission to play. Let them say childish things. Allow them to grieve when they can and how they can. Help them understand they have a heavenly Father who knows them and accepts them as they are—by being an earthly parent who knows and accepts them the same way.

Helping Children Deal With a Loved One's Terminal Illness

- Talk to your children about the stages of the illness and help them know what to expect. Do not hide the fact that your loved one is dying.
- If possible, let the ill person break the news to the child and answer any questions.
- Talk about *anticipatory grief* with your child, explaining that you will all grieve a little at a time before the person dies.
- Be careful children do not become a parent's or younger sibling's caretaker.
- Try to avoid putting all of life on hold.

- Encourage the ill person to make videos and audiotapes and write letters and cards for children to have in the future.

- Gently encourage, but do not force, children to spend time with their loved one. They will have fewer regrets later if they don't pull away out of self-protection now.

- Encourage your children to use time with the ill person to make a memory book of happy times: to reminisce together, write their memories down, add favorite photos, and make drawings.

- Let children be your guide in how involved they want to be in funeral preparations.

- When the loved one dies, expect mixed feelings of profound loss coupled with relief. Let children know that's normal and okay.

Eight Things Not to Say to a Grieving Child

1. "Now you're the 'man of the house'" (or the 'little mother').
2. "You're the rock of the family."
3. "Take it like a soldier."
4. "Don't feel bad."
5. "Don't cry."
6. "You'll get over it."
7. "You should be over this by now."
8. "It's time to move on with your life."

SIX

Listen Without Reacting

Kids in pain can say very hurtful things.

After her parents' divorce, thirteen-year-old Sara told her mom, "If you had been a better wife, Daddy would never have left us. It's all your fault he walked out on us!" Then she slammed the bedroom door behind her. Jan had never seen her daughter act in such a way or heard such hurtful things come out of her mouth.

When I had to tell my sons that their father had leukemia, Tate, who was eleven, said, "Well, God better not let Dad die. I've prayed for him for years. I've prayed every night, at least a million times, for Dad to walk. God hasn't answered that prayer. And I'm telling you, if he lets my dad die, I'm just not going to believe in him anymore. And I mean it!" Then he burst into tears.

Tate's threat shocked me at first. But instead of trying to talk him out of how he felt or giving him a litany of all God had done for us, I just let him cry and express his deep sorrow over the thought of losing his father ... again.

One of the best life supports we can give hurting children is to listen as they express their thoughts and feelings, no matter how hard those thoughts and feelings may be to hear. By listening to them, we can help our children heal.

Encourage Your Child to Talk With You

University of Michigan psychologist Albert Cain, a child bereavement specialist, believes that parents need to say to their children, "This is something we can talk about. It's not too overwhelming for me. I'm not going to dissolve into a sea of tears. I'm not going to shut you up or turn you off. We can talk about this again and again."[1] According to Cain, the goal is to promote periodic conversation, not just a one-time interaction with the child.

Healthy families let children know that they can speak of their parent, whether deceased or divorced, and express their feelings about their loss, as often as they wish. Tell your kids again and again:

"It's okay for you to cry."
"It's okay for Mom (or Dad) to cry."
"It's okay to express our emotions."

Remind your children as well that the intensity of their pain will eventually ebb. Grief is a new experience for children. They may not realize that they won't feel this bad forever. While they will never "get over it," their sorrow will lessen with time.

Roxanne, a divorced mom, observes: "I repeatedly told my three girls not to keep their feelings inside of them, to talk to someone— myself, other family members, someone from church or school, just *someone.*"

Acknowledge Your Child's Feelings

When our children talk to us about their feelings, we need to acknowledge that we've heard and we understand. We can do this even if the child is acting out his or her pain rather than expressing it with words.

While simple, the act of acknowledging another's pain is remarkably effective. When your child expresses grief—whether in words or actions—look that child in the eye and say, "You seem a little sad today," or, "You seem to be angry about something." These words can open a window for communication and can aid in healing.

If it doesn't come naturally to you, ask God to help you become a better listener for your child. Don't be worried that your son or daughter may feel worse if you acknowledge what they are feeling. Just the opposite is true. When we acknowledge pain, fear or other negative emotions, we help others feel understood. This helps them deal with their emotions and move past them.

Validate Your Child's Feelings and Offer Comfort

Your children's honesty about their feelings can be difficult to hear, especially in a divorce when you may feel guilty for inflicting pain on them. But validating your children's feelings is the best antidote for their hurts, and wise parents make a practice of it.

You can validate your children's feelings by saying something like, "Of course you feel sad about your father's illness," or "Of course you're angry about our divorce. It's a very hard thing for you, and I understand why you feel upset about it sometimes." Don't take negative feelings personally or get defensive or react in anger. And don't try to cheer up your children or talk them out of how they feel. Doing so trivializes their pain and makes them feel all the more isolated and lonely. It communicates that you don't really understand the depth of their anguish.

Once your children have expressed their feelings, hold them and sit with them for as long as they want to be held. Rock them and sing to them. Tickle and cuddle them—my ten-year-old still loves to be tickled. Ask them if they have other things they want to talk about. Read to them; most children, of all ages, enjoy being read to. Pray together, talking honestly and conversationally to God about your child and his or her needs.

When Children Don't Talk

Not all children will talk about their feelings, even if the parent is willing to listen. Some of that is temperament, gender or age. Give it time. Your children may be afraid to unload on you when they know you are dealing with your own emotions. Kids will only discuss what they think you can handle or want to hear. If we tell them we want them to talk to us but then disappear into the bedroom and cry, we are sending a mixed message. Kids follow what we do, not what we say. As they see you heal, then they might feel more free.

One of the best ways to find out how someone feels is to tell him or her how *you* feel. It creates safety ... especially with children. Try saying, "I'm feeling sad today," or "I'm feeling lonely without your mom here."

Barbara's husband lived for four months after the diagnosis of his illness, when her two children were teenagers. In the months following his death, Barbara tried to model the honest expression of emotions for her kids. "Even when I was exhausted from either running back and forth to the hospital or taking care of their father at home," she says, "I tried to be as honest with them as I could. I would tell them how I felt—whether I was tired or deeply sad. Now that he's gone, I tell them I miss their dad or that I'm tired of grieving.

My kids know when something's bothering me anyway, and when I talk about my feelings, it seems to help all of us. It helps me grieve, and it tells them that they can grieve as well."

If you feel your child is not talking out of a desire to protect you, which is often the case, encourage him or her to talk to someone else. This could be a relative, a trusted friend, a pastor or a counselor. Christy's mom sent her teenage daughter to see a counselor after Christy was involved in a car accident that left her father in a coma. Christy said she would go only if her mom agreed not to come along; she did not want to burden her mother any further. Mom wisely consented.

"We Forgot to Pray!"
After Tate declared that he no longer believed in God, we sat in the parked car and cried and talked for a long time. But before he climbed out of the car he said, "Wait, Mom! We forgot to pray!" And so we did, and we have continued to pray. Even though Tate did ultimately lose his father to leukemia, he has not lost his faith.

When we listen to our children and model the healthy expression of emotions, we are giving them a life support that will help them survive their pain.

SEVEN

Be Present

Steve's accident happened on the last Sunday in December. I had already sent out invitations to our family's annual New Year's Eve party, but our friends realized the party would be canceled. It didn't occur to me that my children wouldn't make the same assumption.

I had been living at the hospital, waiting, hoping for some response from Steve. My mother, sister and college-age niece had come to Oklahoma City from Dallas to offer me comfort and support during those first few weeks. They were able to care for the boys while I was at the hospital.

In one of my many phone calls home, Jeremy and Tate asked me about the party.

"Oh, we're not having the party," I told them.

"So what are you going to do for New Year's?" Jeremy asked.

"Oh, honey, I'm not planning anything. I'll just be home."

"Oh, good!" the boys cheered in stereo. "Then we can play games together and stay up till midnight. And we can shoot off those poppers you bought for the party. Can we do that, Mom?"

"We'll see," I said. Partying till midnight was the last thing in the world I wanted to do.

That afternoon, alone in the waiting area, I laid my head back against the wall to rest a minute and reflected on my boys' request.

I had hardly seen them the last few days. The thought of going home and playing Yahtzee, popping confetti poppers at midnight and celebrating a New Year sounded awful to me. Yet in the stillness of that waiting room, I sensed God telling me that my sons needed to be with me, if only for an hour or two. The point wasn't to play games with them; it was to give them my presence. Then God whispered something to me I have not forgotten: "*They've lost their father. They don't need to lose their mother, too.*"

I decided then that with God's help I would do everything I could to "be there" for my sons. I didn't know everything that meant; I only knew I needed to do it.

Your Presence Offers Reassurance

Craig's mom died unexpectedly when he and his sister were teens. Before her death, his parents had been planning a move to another state so that his father could return to college. His dad went ahead with the plan. "I really lost my way after that," Craig reflects. "I think it would have helped if Dad had been more available, but he was overwhelmed with his own grief and his schooling."

Craig is right: his father's presence would have helped. "Most adults fail to appreciate the extent to which fear of abandonment exists in all children in every childhood."[1] After Steve's accident, Tate was comfortable going to school, but he didn't want to be left in his Sunday school class or attend soccer practice. He also refused to ride in a separate car from me if we were going places with other people. When I asked him why, he said, "Because if something happens to you, I want to be there to help you." His big brother, knowing there was little a six-year-old would be able to do in an accident, thought this was ridiculous.

Your presence is the most effective way you can counter this kind of fear. "Nothing is as reassuring to your grieving child as your sheer presence. Express your love more frequently, both in words and in hugs and kisses."[2] Spend as much time with your child as possible. This does not mean weekly trips to Disneyland; it means simple, everyday activities. Bake cookies together, read a story together at bedtime, or take a walk together around your neighborhood.

Ask for God's Help to Be Present

Don't wait until you "feel" like spending time with your child. "Children cannot put their lives on hold. For them *now* is what counts."[3] Besides, the very act of *doing* with your child may change your feelings. And if not, you have still done the right thing for your child. "It's your job to reassure your children—by your actions, as well as with words—that even though these are tough times, you're strong enough to be there for them."[4]

If your own grief seems overwhelming, ask God to help you stay available to your children. Tap into his strength as you juggle your feelings and your need to be there for your kids.

Lisa was struggling to regain her balance after her divorce when she felt a nudge from God. "It was almost time to go pick up my son Taylor, who was three at the time," she says. "I had been wounded terribly, but God was showing me that he had my heart, and he was not going to let me down. God helped me to see the truth about myself ... that I had been sitting in the place of sorrow, and that it was time to take my eyes off myself and start caring for the needs of others.

"The first was my son. 'Lord, what could I possibly do with my son that would make him happy after all that he has been through?'

I asked. 'Give him your presence, Lisa. He needs his mommy to love him, hold him and caress him.'

"That evening I did exactly what God asked me to do. I picked Taylor up from his preschool. I went by McDonalds and we took our dinner down to the beach. We sat and ate; we listened to the waves crash along the shoreline, laughed over silly things and made snow angels in the sand. That evening as we were driving home, Taylor said to me, 'Mommy, that was the best time I ever had.'"

I might have wavered in my own commitment to be present for my kids if it hadn't been for my friend Ramona. Ramona's father had died, leaving her mother a widow with four children. Ramona understood what my life was like.

Because her father had been hospitalized in another city, Ramona's mom had had to leave Ramona and her siblings for periods of time. Ramona told me that even though she'd been thirteen at the time, her mother's absence was very hard on her. Ramona reminded me over and over how much my kids needed me. She helped me remember God's whisper in the waiting room.

I can't tell you I was always there for my kids. I wasn't. Nor did I parent them perfectly. I'm sure there were times they needed me and I was not available. I know there were times when I was present in body but not in spirit. But I did make a conscious, deliberate decision to continue to be their parent and to *be present* as much as I could be. I believe as we purpose this in our hearts, God will come alongside us and enable us to do it. For me, it started with a New Year's Eve party of three.

EIGHT

Major on Majors

If you are dealing with an ongoing crisis, you won't be able to carry on as before. You are probably exhausted, particularly if you are trying to do a job that was created for two. You can help your children—and yourself—by deciding what is most important and then letting some things go.

Before Steve's accident I had kept a clean house, but afterwards I spent so much time at the hospital I had little time left to dust or clean. I left beds unmade and dishes unwashed and no longer picked up every night. I didn't prefer to live this way, but I realized that a perfectly clean house was less important than other things I needed to give my family—like my presence!

Some things just have to go because they get in the way of our being able to give kids what they need most. To help your kids stay afloat during this time, you'll need to make it a priority to give your kids what they need. While every child is unique and every crisis presents unique situations and resulting concerns, in general, grieving children require the same things.

Predictability
When everything around them seems topsy-turvy, kids need a level of stability at home. Part of their life needs to remain predictable. Keeping old routines going and keeping changes to a minimum are important in times of crisis.

Keep as many routines as possible. Experts agree that all children need routine. Carrie Lance, a crisis counselor for children in Oklahoma City, says that "when something unexpected happens in a child's life, he needs the expected."[1]

Strive to keep as much of your children's daily routine the same as it was before the trauma: when and how they wake up, what they eat for breakfast, when they get dressed, how they get to school, what they do after school and what they eat after school. Keep the same expectations about homework and TV that you had before the crisis. Most of all, maintain your children's bedtime routine. Don't rush this time. Instead, allow plenty of time for your children to wind down, take baths, read a bedtime story and talk.

Of course you will not be able to maintain all routines all the time. No one can. The point is to strive for predictability. You may have to identify which routines are most important to maintain. I tried to schedule consistent mealtimes and bedtimes and did my best to read and pray with my children before tucking them in for the night.

Minimize changes. You may be tempted to "get out of this house" because it holds painful memories, but this may not be good for your child. In *Helping Children Survive Divorce*, Dr. Archibald Hart says: "If I were to single out the most serious mistake that divorcing parents make, it would be this: you change things too quickly."[2] He says that children are more capable of adapting when change takes place slowly. Divorce, death or serious illnesses and injury can bring tremendous change into the home. Avoiding other changes gives children time to adjust.

If possible, keep your kids in the same house, school and church.

Change only what you must change. If changes need to be made, delay them or spread them out as much as possible, and then try to minimize their impact. If you have to move, try to move to a house that allows your kids to go to the same school and even take the same bus route.

Most experts recommend that parents wait six months to a year before making any major changes if the family has experienced loss. When you do have to make a change, talk to your children about it ahead of time. Remember that keeping them informed helps them to stay afloat.

While most of the time it's best to avoid change, at times change is good. For example, Mike lost his wife, Debbie, to cancer while he was senior pastor at their church. Debbie had been diagnosed soon after the couple had taken the assignment. They spent eighteen months battling the disease before Debbie died. Both sets of grandparents as well as aunts, uncles and cousins lived in another state, and Mike did not feel he could carry on as senior pastor and take care of their children.

Within three months of Debbie's death, Mike had found a staff position at another church and moved his children near his extended family. While it went against conventional wisdom, three years later Mike is convinced it was the right thing for all of them.

Time to Adjust and Regain Balance

Adults who experience a loss through divorce or death may need from six months to two years before life begins to feel somewhat normal. During this time they often feel dazed and "crazy." One widow expressed surprise when she discovered that the second year after her husband's death was more difficult than the first.

Children, too, need time to adjust to the changes in their family. It helps to know how your children may react to the stress in your family. Common reactions may include

- Shock, surprise and disbelief
- Worry about how their world will change
- Sadness and loneliness
- Shame and feeling different
- Anger at both parents
- Confusion over loyalty[3]

You may also see:

- *Hyperactivity.* During the months following a death or divorce children often have difficulty concentrating. Some may appear to "bounce off the walls," unable to sit still. Others daydream and seem lost in their own world. My son Tate became super silly and hyper after his dad's accident. I remember once crossing a busy street with him, terrified he was going to get away from me and run into the traffic.

- *Poor grades.* Your children's grades may suffer for a time. They may miss a day or two of school as they struggle to come to grips with what has happened, particularly if they did not expect the crisis. This is normal and necessary—and most likely temporary. They need your support and understanding.

Times of Fun and Laughter

Laughter is great therapy for adults. Since play is part of childhood, it may be even more therapeutic for kids. In order to ensure that your kids and you share fun times together, you need to plan these times into your week.

Because our weeks were fairly scheduled with school, homework and church activities, I tried to set aside time each weekend for fun. We often checked the Dollar Theater for movies that were appropriate. Both boys played Little League sports through our church and we all attended their games where there were lots of friends and families to socialize with.

My friend Susan, whose husband's work often took him out of town, found the best deals on eating out. On Thursday evenings a local fish place offered two free children's dinners for every adult meal purchased. On Tuesday nights a local drive-in offered hamburgers for half price. Susan or I sometimes picked up the burgers and then met up with our kids at a park or at one of our homes. This gave me time with another adult, the boys had friends to play with, and the cost was little more than eating at home.

Jackie and her girls happened upon an idea that proved to be so satisfying for all of them that Ellen and Amanda requested it over and over through the years. Jackie would rent several movies, make a pallet in the living room and fix a fondue. She and the girls would eat dinner and then watch videos till the wee hours of the morning until they all fell asleep on the living room floor together. Jackie says that the soreness in her back was a small sacrifice for the wealth of fun memories this time gave her with her girls.

Karen's husband, Ted, was diagnosed with an arterial vascular malformation, or AVM (a mass of malformed veins in his brain stem) nine years ago. An operation to remove the mass left extensive damage to the area around the AVM, causing a stroke-like outcome that impaired Ted's ability to walk, see, hear, swallow, blink his eyes or speak clearly. His right side is completely numb and he is now confined to a wheelchair. "One of the most therapeutic things we do as a family," says Karen, "is to visit Ted's relatives about twice a year. When we get in the car and get away from this house all our spirits improve. Ted shows us the places he spent his boyhood and tells jokes. It's some of the best times we have."

Once the initial shock has worn off from a family crisis, encourage your children to play with their friends and to do the activities they did before the crisis. Remember that this is the only childhood your children will ever have. It's okay to laugh again.

As you work to regain your balance when life has sent you reeling, ask God for wisdom to help you decide what the majors in your family need to be. He knows your temperament, your energy level and your stress load. He also knows your children. Depend on him to guide you in staying afloat.

NINE

Keep Them Connected

It was an overcast Sunday morning and Paula was dead tired. A newly single mom with two school-age girls, she taught kindergarten five days a week and used Saturdays to catch up on household chores and errands. Before her ten-year marriage ended, Paula had been a stay-at-home mom, and it would never have occurred to her to sleep in and miss church. But today …

Besides, how nice it would be not to have to face all those intact families walking into the sanctuary. She could avoid the problem of where to sit and who to sit with. Mostly, she would not have to feel like a modern-day Hester Prynne, walking in with a scarlet D written across her forehead. Yes, there were lots of reasons for staying home today.

Just as she rolled over to go back to sleep, Amy and Tracy came bounding into her room. "Get up, Mom, it's time for church. Get up or we'll be late," they cried.

"Hey, girls," she said as she grabbed them and pulled them into bed with her. "How about we stay home this morning? I'll read us a Bible story and we'll sing some songs. We'll have church at home!" Paula sold it like she was a used car salesman.

"And not see our friends?" asked Tracy, horrified.

"We're having an attendance contest with the boys," said Amy, "and if I'm not there the girls might lose. We've got to go!"

In that brief interchange, Paula saw how important going to church was for her daughters. She had no idea that they would mount such a protest. But as she dragged herself out of bed, she realized that maybe they all needed church in a different way than they had before her divorce.

When we are suffering, we feel like hiding behind a wall and taking our children with us. While time alone to process our grief is important, we need to strike a healthy balance. We need to stay connected—particularly, if at all possible, with our children's other parent.

Staying Connected With a Non-Custodial Parent

Don's two sons, who are now grown, tell him that it helped them tremendously to have both parents in their lives and to see how Don worked with their mother to make sure that happened. Experts agree: "Divorcing parents must realize that the most loving gift they can give to their children is permission to be as close to the other parent as to themselves."[1] Do your best to talk with your spouse about how you can work together to help your children say afloat through the storm of divorce.

Marty and Linda divorced when their sons were seven and nine. It was difficult at first, but they were both committed to providing a united front to their sons. They went out of their way to support each other and encourage their sons' relationships with the other parent. Linda kept the boys during the week, and Marty had them on weekends and for a couple of weeks during the summer. Both were very involved in their sons' lives.

If your children's non-custodial parent lives in a different area than you do, try to keep them in touch with their long-distance parent. Encourage your ex-spouse to:

- Call your child often
- Write and send cards and other surprises in the mail (these do not have to be expensive)
- Use e-mail
- Tape record messages or stories for young children
- Visit frequently

On your end, help your child to reciprocate with calls, letters and other forms of communication. Remind yourself you are not doing this for your ex, you are doing it for your child.

Stay Connected Socially

I pulled into the baseball field parking lot. We had not been to a field since the year before when Steve had been coaching. Tate jumped out of the car and ran to meet his teammates and his other coach, Bill, who also happened to be a lifelong friend of Steve's. I wept at the picture of a team without my husband coaching, but Tate didn't seem to notice. He was too excited about the start of a new season. I was glad he had familiar friends and coaches to connect with.

One of the easiest things to drop in a single-parent home is social activities. The parent is usually struggling to get his or her children's basic needs met, let alone any extras. But if your kids remain involved in church activities, scouts, sports or music, they will get some important needs met: they'll have fun and retain a level of predictability and normalcy—plus they'll get a break from you and the sadness all of you are feeling.

Sometimes children find comfort just hanging around adults whom they know to be safe and caring, perhaps watching TV together with a family friend or going out back to feed the birds with grandpa. Little ones can find comfort cuddling in the lap of a caring adult.

Two weeks after Steve died, our neighbor invited us to her daughter's annual birthday party. Lots of families and kids would be there, and Tate and Katelyn wanted to go. I was not in a partying mood and told the kids I did not feel like being with people. Tate, eleven years old at the time, said, "It helps me to be with people, Mom. Then I don't feel so sad." I was thankful Tate was able to verbalize his feelings. He was so eager to go to the party that he offered to take Katelyn and attend without me.

Your kids may be able to talk to people in your community in ways they can't with you, in part because they are fearful of burdening you further with their own pain. If there are others in their lives who will listen—an aunt, a teacher, a friend—they may be more willing to talk about what they are experiencing.

Sometimes a trusted peer can help your child grieve. One night when Jeremy was thirteen, he had a friend sleep over. They set up a board game in my walk-in closet and played for hours. Later, my son told me that he and Brett had done a lot more than play Monopoly. They had talked about Steve and all he had been through. Jeremy might never have unloaded on me, but he felt safe enough to tell a friend some of his struggles.

Stay Connected With Extended Family

As much as possible, keep your kids connected to both parents' families. This connection is critical for keeping your kids afloat. "The loss of special family members and important relationships is extremely damaging, for children need a family. For their children's sake, parents should make every effort to preserve and foster all of a child's familial relationships, no matter how angry or upset they may be with the other parent and the other parent's family."[2]

When Jackie realized that she would have to end her marriage for her girls' sake, she made a deliberate decision not to end their ties with her husband's family. "I tried to keep separated mine and Frank's issues. I stayed connected with Frank's family. I had to put their needs ahead of mine, and I knew they needed those relationships. For years the girls have spent one evening a week with Frank's sister."

Bill's wife, Connie, died, leaving Bill to father their one child, Krista, a fifteen-year-old sophomore in high school. Several months after Connie's death, Bill arranged for his in-laws, Krista and himself to take a trip to visit aunts, uncles and cousins living in other states. It was a beneficial time for all of them. Staying connected to her mother's family helped Krista still feel connected to her mom. Bill demonstrated to Krista that even though she had lost her mother, she did not have to lose grandparents, aunts and uncles.

Ami's husband, Fred, was killed when their three children were four, six and eleven. Ami worked four days a week and desperately needed help with childcare and the logistics of a busy family. Her children were involved in gymnastics, Bible quizzing and many other activities. Family members stepped in to help Ami, caring for her preschool son and chauffeuring her kids. Fred's sister and husband even relocated and bought a house in Ami's neighborhood so they could be close enough to fill in for her. The family's practical support made a tremendous difference for Ami and her children. While dealing with their loss, her children were able to continue on with many of the things that had defined their life before their dad's death.

When Ami's husband died, both of their families closed ranks around her and her children. But what do you do when you do not have this kind of system in place? What if your family lives too far away or is not able to support you in a practical way?

If you don't live near family, do your best to encourage those relationships through phone calls or e-mails and regular visits. You can also enlist people to fill in the gaps.

Finding People to Fill in the Gap

To consciously develop other adult resources, begin asking the people who already make up your child's "natural communities"—family, teachers, youth and scout leaders and coaches.

Here are some ways to do this:

- Ask adults to help your child. Most adults care. They'll jump if you give them specific ways to help. I called my artistic friend, Angela, when Tate needed last-minute help with a poster for school. Her husband Bill came to Tate's rescue when I told him about Tate's struggles on a baseball team. Our friend Terry worked with the boys on getting their miniature wooden cars ready for the Pinewood Derby. We called Tate's Sunday school teacher when he needed an adult mentor for a yearlong project in the eighth grade. My neighbor Stan even came over one night at 10:30 to get a wasp out of the boys' bedroom! (God had taught me to ask!)

- Educate the adults in your child's life about children's grief (from death, illness or divorce) and how they can help. Give them books/articles to read. Suggest ways to start conversations with your child: to share memories ("I remember when ..."), to share personal thoughts ("I miss ...") or to acknowledge their feelings ("You seem sad today ...").

- Be a model for other adults about how to communicate with children in an honest way. You do this by talking openly and freely about your own feelings.

- Teach your child to ask for what he or she needs. Let your child know that it's okay to talk about feelings with teachers at school or church or to ask to see a counselor or nurse.

- Reinforce helpful behaviors in caring adults. Adults like affirmation as much as children do. Catch adults in the act of supporting your child well. Compliment them, if possible in front of others.

- Advocate for your child over the years. Remember, teachers and coaches change. Don't hesitate to inform adults in your child's life each year of the challenges they have dealt with in the past.

Especially for Boys

Nowhere is help more needed than in a home where a boy has lost his father, whether by death, abandonment, divorce or abuse. In such instances, boys need male mentors. "The caring attention of a male adult can serve to mitigate the damage to a boy after the death of his father.... Infants, grade-schoolers, and adolescents all seemed to accommodate their loss more readily when a man took a special interest in them in the months and years that followed the death."[3]

Dr. James Dobson, psychologist, author and founder of Focus on the Family, recommends that single moms get a grandpa, uncle or other family member to spend time with fatherless sons.

Debbie was concerned about her son when she left her husband, who had a problem with alcohol and drugs. She realized that Taylor, who has three sisters and no brothers, was going to be living in an all-female household. She asked God to bring some men into her son's life, and he did. One of the associate pastors at their church took Taylor under his wing. He took Taylor to car shows and out golfing. Debbie says that Taylor knows more about cars than she does or ever will. She is so thankful God provided Pastor Doug for her son at such a crucial time in his life.

If no one comes forward from your circle of communities, consider "hiring" a buddy—a trusted, mature high school or college boy to hang out with your son. Of course, you will need to thoroughly screen anyone you hire.

After my husband's accident, my older son, Jeremy, had several close friends whose fathers invested great amounts of time in him and his younger brother Tate. They frequently took the boys out for pizza, invited them to spend the night or took them camping. But as Jeremy grew older, I felt he needed more time with these men without his little brother tagging along. At the same time, I felt that Tate needed a strong male influence more than ever.

So I placed an ad at our local Christian college and eventually hired a freshman to play with Tate a couple of afternoons a week. Scott was on a baseball scholarship (Tate's favorite sport), so he played catch with him and took him to the batting cages. Tate loved to roller blade, so they would go to the campus with its maze of sidewalks and ramps to skate. Sometimes Scott stayed for dinner. Other times he took Tate to the college cafeteria for its "all you can eat" evening meal. Tate was in heaven. Scott was a fine Christian young man with the added bonus of being very respectful and polite. He always said, "Yes, Ma'am" and "No, Ma'am." Not a bad role model for my nine-year-old.

The relationship was good for both of them. Tate got a big brother who concentrated on him and his favorite activities each week, things I could not do nor would I have time for. Scott got a pretty good deal too. I used to tease him about how he had the best job on campus—he was paid to play and he got a few home-cooked meals thrown in too.

God's perfect plan was for a family to have a mother and a father. Because we live in a fallen world, many of us do not live in this model. Raising children has never been harder, and raising children alone is impossible. That's why you shouldn't do it alone, especially if you are a single mom with a boy. Let family members, friends, the body of Christ help you. If they don't offer, ask. Your child's best chance to stay afloat is with the help of others holding him up.

A Better View of Divorce

"Promise your kids two parents after the divorce. The best help parents can give children is to let them know that each parent deserves a space in their lives."[4] Although divorced, you are still a family—a separated family, but still a family.

- See your ex as the co-parent of your child, not your ex-spouse.

- Develop a sense of teamwork with your ex. Even if you don't feel like a team, continue to act like one. It's best for your child.

- Realize you are not the only parent your child needs. Children do best when the relationship with both parents is strong.

TEN

Preserve Memories, Make New Traditions

Children need their parents—both of them. When they lose a parent permanently through death or partially through divorce, illness or injury, we need to encourage them at least to keep their memories.

For the many months Steve was in the hospital and then after he died, I made a conscious effort to talk about him with my children. We relived the vacation in Colorado when we'd left a Wendy's restaurant totally embarrassed because we were all laughing so hard our food was coming out of our mouths. We recalled the many bike rides we had taken, playing follow-the-leader. We reveled in Steve's spontaneity, like the time he tried to follow Jeremy's wayward helium balloon or when he stopped the car in a deserted parking lot to help four-year-old Tate find his imaginary pet mouse, "Mouser." Talking about Steve both kept him real and kept his memory alive for my children and me.

Remembering With Photos

One of the best ways to preserve memories is through photographs of our loved ones. Encourage children to look at pictures of the parent they've lost, and use the photos as springboards for remembering good times with that parent. When Jeremy turned twelve and Steve was still hospitalized, I made a photo album that contained pictures of just Jeremy and his father. It became a cherished keepsake. Years later, Tate followed suit and created one for himself, pulling pictures from our various albums of just him and his dad.

One father I know put together a framed collage of his children with their deceased mother. Another father, Mike, had taken a picture of Debbie with their children every Mother's Day. Before she passed away, he collected those pictures and put them into a Mother's Day album.

Sometimes after a painful divorce, the last thing you want to look at is a picture of your former spouse staring at you. But remember this person is still your children's parent. At least allow your kids to keep a picture in their rooms and have an album available. One of my friends lost her father when she was nine. Within a year her mother remarried and she and her siblings were not allowed to have any pictures of their dad in the house. She still recalls the pain of having to give up another part of her father.

Remembering Through Memory Boxes

Memory boxes are another good way to preserve memories. Although these are usually created after a person has died, a memory box could also be helpful to children after a parent is lost through divorce or abandonment.

You might buy a special box, but a simple shoebox will also work. The idea is to place items that belonged to or remind the child of the parent: photos, jewelry, hobby items, small pieces of clothing such as a favorite tie or scarf, programs or ticket stubs from events attended together. Let your mind run free. A memory box can even be a project you do with your children. If the parent is still living, your child can add to the memory box over time. The important thing is to permit children to keep their memories.

Keeping Traditions

When someone is missing from the family, we may have to adjust our family traditions, but it is helpful to hang onto as many of them as we can.

Aly's family always enjoyed a weekly Family Movie Night. They rented a video, ate popcorn mixed with M&M's and drank pop. After Aly's mom died, they stopped this tradition until a counselor working with Aly and her dad encouraged them to resume it. Although she was nineteen, Aly continued to need that family time.

Family traditions can involve recreation and hobbies, church activities, foods, prayer and devotional times. One mother had always gathered her children around her every morning for a prayer before sending them off to school. After her divorce, this prayer time became an even more significant daily tradition, giving the entire family added strength to deal with their needs as well as a tie to each other that carried them through the day.

Holidays and Other Special Days

Nowhere are children's memories more vivid than around holidays. After experiencing a major loss, many parents dread special days such as Thanksgiving, Christmas, anniversaries, birthdays, Mother's Day and Father's Day. And with good reason. These events can trigger increased sadness and make us feel exceptionally lonely. It is helpful to remember that the first year of holidays following a loss is usually the hardest. Also, many parents report that the anticipation of the event can be worse than the actual day itself.

Despite how we may feel, our kids need to celebrate special occasions and maintain holiday traditions. Just as with daily routines, children find solace in keeping the customs of special days, even when so much else has changed.

My friend Cheri recalls her family's first Christmas after her father died. He had always loved real Christmas trees, and that's all she and her five siblings had ever known. Her mother mistakenly thought it would be good for all of them to have a new start. She brought home a white artificial tree and pink ornaments. The children wept when they saw the tree. Not only was their father gone, but now his tradition was gone as well. The next year they brought back the evergreen and their memories.

Talk with your kids about what to expect during upcoming holidays. Discuss their feelings and expectations. If they will be dividing their time between two homes, tell them about the arrangements.

If you are dealing with a death, talk about the traditions you want to keep. Before Fred died, Ami's family had always participated in their town's annual Christmas tree auction. The family would choose a theme for their tree and decorate it. The trees were then sold and the money donated to the local library. The Christmas after Fred died, Ami and her kids poured themselves into their project. It proved to be an important tradition to keep for her children, giving them a connection with their dad now that he was gone. The tradition also helped keep them tied to a community they had all enjoyed. Every year as they work on their tree, Ami and her children talk about the previous trees they have done, and it becomes a time of remembering.

Birthdays and anniversaries offer opportunities to remember and honor a parent who has died. Turn your loss into something positive by using the day to tell stories about your loved one, to eat the person's favorite foods, or to engage in his or her favorite activities.

One year on the date of Steve's birthday, I invited three families who were close to him over for a meal. Beforehand, I asked the adults to think of their favorite "Steve stories" to tell my children. When the meal was over, we gathered in the family room to hear their stories. My kids listened as our friends took turns telling their tales. Not only did this help keep their memory of their dad alive, it helped them feel good about the kind of man he was and helped them see the impact he'd had on those around him.

You can do something similar through photographs and videos. Some families mark the anniversary of a parent's death by looking through albums or watching home videos.

If one parent has died, ask your kids how they would like to spend the anniversary of the death. "On the first year anniversary of my husband's death, I gathered the family together and asked them what they thought Dad would want us to do to remember him," says Deb. "It didn't take long for a decision: get White Castle hamburgers, take lounge chairs, and sit at the grave recollecting stories about Dad and telling jokes (something he really liked doing). We even invited our pastor and other family members to join us. What a healing day!"

As she approached the one-year anniversary of her husband's death, Barb talked to each of her three children about how they would like to mark it. Her two older sons both wanted to spend the night with friends and just treat it as a regular day. Barb allowed them that freedom. She and her ten-year-old daughter went away for the evening to a bed and breakfast. They spent a lot of time talking about their memories and found it a meaningful night. Barb wisely asked her kids for input and allowed them some control over how to spend the day.

While these activities come more naturally for parents following a death, you can help your children through a divorce by encouraging them to remember a parent's birthday or other significant days. Help them make or select cards or gifts. Encourage them to spend time with the parent on that special day or at least to talk with him or her on the phone. One mother told me about a bouquet of flowers being delivered to her office on her birthday. To her surprise she found it was from her ex-husband with a note thanking her for being such a good mother to their daughter. Gestures like these are powerful statements to children and give them the freedom they need to love both parents.

Create New Rituals

May Ann and James Emswiler, authors of *Guiding Your Child Through Grief*, recommend creating new rituals with children. First, rituals use actions, a means of expression that is much more familiar and comfortable for kids than words. Second, good rituals enable children to participate as much or as little as they wish. Third, because rituals have a beginning and an end, children know they will only be confronting their pain for a short time. And fourth, rituals that are repeated feel safe to children because they know what to expect.[1]

Rituals can be planned or spontaneous. Here are some ideas for rituals you might consider:

Christmas:
- Read your loved one's favorite Christmas story out loud or watch a favorite video.
- Give a gift of time or money to a charity in memory of the deceased parent.

- For each of your children, wrap a gift of something that belonged to the missing parent. (This can be repeated for years.)
- Light a candle during mealtime, or along with the Advent candles, in memory of your loved one.

Birthdays or anniversaries:
- Let each child make a memory box containing small belongings of the deceased parent.
- Plant a tree or a flower garden in honor of the missing parent. Memorialize it with a stone or plaque.
- Put together a photo album or scrapbook of your loved one.
- Bake a cake on the person's birthday to celebrate his or her life.

Be Flexible

Some families find that when they face holidays without their loved one, they need a complete change of scenery. Make sure you talk with your kids about this before making plans. If you normally go to Grandmother's house on Thanksgiving and stay at home for Christmas, you might try reversing it. If it's possible to take a trip, you might find that the fun of travel would be a pleasant diversion during the holidays. Some single parent homes can feel "empty" during these days. Perhaps you know another single parent family you could invite over to share your celebration. This is a way to help yourself as well as someone else during a difficult time.

These are just a few ideas to help you jump-start your family to find ways to deal with holidays and other special occasions. The truth is, holidays will never be the same—nor will we. But if we can hang on to traditions that bind us together while creating new ones that help us move along in our grief journey, we will find another support to help us stay afloat.

ELEVEN

Point Them to the Father

After twenty-three months of hospitalization, Steve returned to our home confined to a wheelchair. Every night as I tucked Tate into his bottom bunk, he prayed for his dad to walk again. While Steve's brain injury left him with short-term memory loss and speech difficulties, the one disability that concerned Tate was his walking. Often, after prayer, Tate would ask:

"Why can't Daddy walk?"

"Because when he had the wreck his brain got hurt. It hurt the part of his brain that makes his legs move," I answered.

"Can't God heal him?"

"Yes, he could," I would reply. "God has the power to do that, but he hasn't."

"Why?" Tate would counter.

"I don't know."

"Couldn't he do a miracle?"

"Yes, he could, Tate. But God doesn't always do miracles."

"Why?"

"I don't know."

"Doesn't he love Daddy?"

"Yes, he does. But God doesn't stop all bad things from happening on earth. He gave people the ability to choose to do good or bad. When we choose to do bad, it hurts ourselves and others." I tried to explain my theology as well as I could in eight-year-old terms.

"Like when Paul drank and then drove his car. He hit Daddy."

"Yes, that's exactly right. We wish God would stop all bad stuff, but he hasn't yet. He will one day, and that's what heaven will be. No bad stuff ever again. Until then, bad things do happen, even to those who believe. Just look at Jesus. God loved him, and yet bad things happened in his life."

"I know." Tate snuggled down with a yawn. "I just wish God would make my daddy walk again. He still could, you know."

"I know. Goodnight, Tate," I said as I kissed him and left the room.

I had few answers for Tate. I still don't. There are no pat answers for tragedy. There is nothing we can say or do that will make it all go away. So what can we give children to hold on to when we have no answers? We must hand them the things we know to be true about God and then pray they will take hold through the storm.

While there is much we don't know, there are some things we do know and must tell our kids: God loves them, and he will provide.

"God Loves You"

Children need to know that God loves them. Kids who have been taken to church or Sunday school have heard this all their lives, but they may not actually believe it. They need to be convinced of its truth. How can you help?

Teach them to pray it. When I was a college student, our campus pastor told us she was going to teach us a prayer to pray. "It's so simple," she said, "you'll be tempted to discount it. But if you'll pray it, it will change your life." The prayer was, "Lord, teach me that you love me." I took the challenge and began to pray those words as often as they came to mind. Over time, I began to recognize that I had begun to internalize all the head knowledge I had about God's love for me into a deeply held heart-truth. Thirty years later, when I faced the biggest crisis of my life, I knew that God loved Steve, my kids and myself. It was not a struggle. Our children can have this same confidence in God and in his love for them if they begin to pray this prayer.

When I began praying that God would teach my children that he loved them, I didn't expect instant results. I knew I was planting a seed, and that God would cultivate the truth inside each of them. At times I saw the seed I'd planted taking root.

Ten days before Steve's accident, the boys and I had bundled up to deliver our Angel Tree gifts at the local drop-off point. Angel Tree is a project of Chuck Colson's Prison Fellowship that provides Christmas gifts for children whose parents are incarcerated. It was raining hard, so I threw an umbrella and my Bible in the car. Jeremy and Tate were excited to be setting out for an adventure on a stormy night.

When we arrived, the rain hammered the roof of our car. While we waited for the storm to let up, I turned in my Bible to Matthew 25 and read aloud the parable of the sheep and the goats. Trying to be heard over the noise outside, I loudly explained to the boys that what we were doing was more than just taking the toys and clothes we had just purchased and leaving them in an office. According to Matthew 25, when we feed the hungry or give a cup to the thirsty, we literally give to God. I also explained that Scripture tells us to visit those in prison, and that this was also a way that we as a family could minister to a prisoner.

I wasn't sure how much of this message got through—it's hard to compete with an Oklahoma thunderstorm. Eventually the rain stopped and we splashed our way into the building to leave our offerings.

Ten days later, with Steve's accident, our family life took a dramatic turn. Our home teemed with visitors, flowers and casseroles, but amidst all the activity, Jeremy pulled me back to the bedroom and shut the door.

"Mom," he questioned, "why are all these people being so nice to us? Is it because of Dad's accident?"

"Well, yes, Jeremy," I responded. "They're trying to do what they can to help and support us during this time."

He looked reflective. "So ... is this our cup of water?"

For a moment I didn't follow him. Then I realized that he was referring to the parable in Matthew.

"Why, yes ... yes it is," I said, marveling at my young son's insight.

When I had read that scripture, I had hoped it would be a teaching moment, an opportunity to make Christmas more meaningful. Little did I know that God had something else in mind. I could not have known that we would soon be trading places with a prisoner's child, that we would be on the receiving end of others' generosity. Nor would I have dreamed that my child would need to apply God's word in a deeper, more personal way to his own life once Christmas was over.

Plant the seeds of God's love. It will bloom when your child needs it.

Pray over your children ... often and repeatedly. "Lord, teach my children that you love them." Pray this prayer daily for your kids. Pray this prayer as they leave for school or go to their other parent's for the weekend; as you drop them off for soccer practice or take them to the hospital to see a dying grandparent. Pray this prayer as you tuck them into bed for the night. It makes a difference.

As you begin to teach this and pray this for your child, check to see if you believe it yourself. If not, pray it for yourself as well. When we are assured of God's love for us we can say with confidence, "I don't know why this has happened to us, but I know this: God loves us." With that assurance comes peace and rest in the midst of turmoil.

Teach Your Children That God Provides

When children begin to believe that God loves them, they'll find it easier to believe that God will provide for them. Scripture is full of God's promises to care for us:

- "But you, O God, do see trouble and grief ... you are the helper of the fatherless" (Ps 10:14).
- "A father to the fatherless, a defender of widows, is God in his holy dwelling. God sets the lonely in families ..." (Ps 68:5-6a).
- "He upholds the cause of the oppressed and gives food to the hungry. The Lord watches over the alien and sustains the fatherless and the widow" (Ps 146:7, 9).
- "For I know the plans I have for you," declares the Lord, "plans to prosper you and not to harm you, plans to give you hope and a future" (Jer 29:11)
- "I will repay you for the years the locusts have eaten.... You will have plenty to eat, until you are full, and you will praise the name of the Lord your God, who has worked wonders for you" (Jl 2:25-26).

- "And my God will meet all your needs according to his glorious riches in Christ Jesus" (Phil 4:19).
- "…put their hope in God, who richly provides us with everything for our enjoyment" (1 Tm 6:17b).

Read these passages together with your kids. Write them out and hang them where your children will see them frequently: on the bathroom mirror, on the kitchen cabinet, in the kids' lockers. The words can serve as constant reminders of God's care. Pray and ask God to help you really believe these promises for your life.

Together begin a family prayer journal in which you list your needs: test on Tuesday, tires for the car, etc. Then record how God answers. Ellen says this is one of the most dramatic ways God has shown himself to her and her family since her husband's tragic accident. Countless times they were in need of something and together they prayed for it and waited to see how God would answer.

When Ellen's daughter turned sixteen, she needed a car. The car she wanted was too expensive, and she was deeply disappointed and frustrated. Ellen encouraged Chelle to continue to pray and wait on God. Four months later they found the very same car, in good running condition but in desperate need of some tender loving care cosmetically. The price was exactly what they could afford. Chelle's faith soared as she realized God cared for her personally and had provided for her.

Jill's husband left her and their twins when the boys were twelve. The couple had been separated for a year when he came home one night to announce he was ending the marriage. Her sons cried themselves to sleep, but Jill lay awake all night, asking the Lord for wisdom and strength. Since they had been toddlers, she'd had a ritual of awakening the boys each morning with their own original song. The past year she had rarely been able to find the strength to sing to them. But the morning following her husband's announcement, Jill found her voice again. The boys greeted their mom's wake-up song with sheepish grins that had been missing from their faces for months. Then one of them spoke up: "God put our song back in your heart, Mom. We're going to be all right now, because we're not alone. He's going to take care of us." That was seven years ago and the twins are now in college and doing well. God did provide.

When Steve had his accident, his car was totaled. My car was fifteen years old and had 150,000 miles on it, and we had been saving for a van. In the months that followed the accident, between trips to the hospital and the boys' activities I found myself almost living in my old car. I worried about it breaking down and wondered if I should buy a new one, although the thought of making such a major purchase without Steve was overwhelming.

Steve's closest friend, Mark, offered to help me look for another car. He "happened" upon an incredible deal on a van and met me to test drive it. Later that evening he called to encourage me to make my decision soon, for he did not feel the van would be there long. After I hung up the phone I whispered a prayer: "God, I just wish I knew what to do ... what you want me to do ... what Steve would want me to do." Pulling open a file drawer, I saw a folder marked "VAN." I opened it and found copies of *Consumer Reports* on mini-vans. Then I remembered that a month before Steve's accident he had done some research and had actually found a van for sale that he had considered buying. He had decided at the time that it would be better to wait and save some more.

Underneath the magazine articles there was a yellow piece of paper with some notes on it in Steve's handwriting. In astonishment, I read about the van he had looked at six months earlier. The minivan he almost bought was feature-for-feature like the one I had test driven earlier that day. The only difference was that the one I had driven had about fifty thousand less miles on it. I called Mark back immediately. I had my answer. I knew what Steve would want me to do.

If our kids know that God loves them and that he provides for his children, they will have a strong raft to support them in their family crisis.

Music helps us rise above. One practical way to help your children focus on the Father is to fill your life with music. You can do this at home or in the car. Music has a way of giving our hearts wings and helping us momentarily to rise above our struggles.

Music has been a helpful resource for Elizabeth and her three children. "Satan can make me feel responsible for this tragedy," she says. "He can pull my kids down to sadness. I have found the best way to keep him out of my house is first to pray and then to listen to praise music. My kids have definitely found an oasis in music."

Be on the lookout for Jesus. Talk to your children about finding God in the everyday. While you may feel sad or angry in response to your loss, one way to get beyond your own emotions is to be on the lookout for God. With young children, make it a game, as if they were detectives. Ask them to report back to you at the end of the day

- When someone was nice or kind to them
- A time they felt happy

- Their favorite part of the day
- If they noticed something in God's creation that was beautiful

You and your children can think of other suggestions. Take time to pray and thank God for showing himself to your child that day. Again, don't expect instant results. View this exercise as a retraining of your minds. "Fix your thoughts on what is true and good and right" (Phil 4:8, LB).

Don't worry if you don't have all the answers for the hard questions your children ask. None of us do. We can't know everything ... but we can know God. Make knowing the truth about God a priority in your family and you will have a life support to lean on that will never sink.

TWELVE

Get Help When You Need It

Shenae and her children, five-year-old Tyler and four-month-old Brady, were doing routine afternoon errands when a car ran a stoplight and smashed broadside into their van. After rolling two-and-a-quarter turns, the van ended up lying on its side, driver's side down. Shenae, conscious but dazed, remembers people pulling the two children out of the backseat while firefighters took forty minutes using the Jaws of Life to pull her from the car. Meanwhile, strangers held her two sons on the side of the road as they watched their mother's rescue.

As Shenae healed physically, she realized that Tyler was going to need some help dealing with the trauma of the accident. Shenae met with a local counselor who came highly recommended from a friend. The counselor told her to explain to Tyler that just as she took him to a doctor when his body was sick, she was going to take him to a "feelings doctor" to help him talk about his feelings after the wreck. Tyler met with the counselor, who used art and play to help him express his feelings about what he had seen.

Shenae's decision to ask for professional help gave her more confidence about how Tyler was handling the trauma of the accident, and she noticed that he seemed less troubled afterward.

Sometimes we can see that our children need something we cannot give them. Sometimes they need more than friends and family can offer. While loved ones can give us emotional and practical support when we allow them, some situations require more than that. How do you know when your children need extra help in dealing with grief and loss?

Most experts agree that occasional problems don't usually require special attention, but ongoing, repeated difficulties that interfere with a child's daily functioning do. The syndrome is called "complicated mourning," and the Child Bereavement Study found that 36 percent of children display symptoms troubling enough to seek professional help.[1] Even when such problems persist, the experts encourage parents not to panic; with a little outside help, most cases can be resolved just as Tyler's was.

Complicating Circumstances

In their book *Guiding Your Child Through Grief,* the Emswilers list several circumstances which may make complicated mourning more likely:

- *Traumatic circumstances.* If your child has witnessed—or received the details of—an unusual event such as a murder, suicide, violent accident, or natural disaster, he or she may need outside help to work through it. Also, abuse of any kind is traumatic and usually requires counseling.

- *Surviving/custodial parent not doing well.* If a child's environment remains chaotic after a traumatic event and the child receives little or no support for mourning, then additional support is helpful. One mother, after suddenly losing her husband in a fiery helicopter crash, sequestered herself in her bedroom for days, coming out only to attend the funeral. Her only child was impacted not only by her father's death but by her mother's inability to deal with it.

- *Love/hate relationship with the parent who is absent.* If a home is disrupted by drug use, alcoholism, abuse, incest, or a bitter divorce battle, children experience conflicted emotions. On one hand they are sad that the family has been separated, on the other they feel relief to be out of the chaos. Their mixed response can cause children to feel guilty, and they may need help sorting out, validating and accepting their feelings.

- *Series of losses.* When your child experiences multiple losses one after the other, he or she will have more difficulty coping. When Cheri was ten, a beloved aunt drowned. Then her grandfather died, and soon after, her father died. At the end of the school year the family moved. Before the year was out, her mother remarried her father's best friend and business partner. Cheri said it wasn't just her father's death that traumatized her and her siblings, but the string of losses.

- *A significant person in a child's life is injured or ill for an extended period.* When all attention and resources have to be channeled to the sick person, a family is put on hold. Children can easily get lost in the shuffle.

- *The child is dealing with other mental health issues in addition to the loss.* Some of these may include childhood depression, anxiety, or ADD/ADHD.[2]

If any of these circumstances are present in your situation (or in the lives of children you know), be sensitive and aware of how the kids are doing. Even though children may not be able to verbalize that they need help in order to stay afloat, you can look for red flags that indicate help is needed.

Warning Signals

Some of the red flags that may indicate a child needs additional help:

- *Changes in personality* at home, in school, in athletics or with friends. For example, a child suddenly hides out in her room or becomes overly clingy and dependent, loses friends because she cannot get along with anyone or has prolonged mood swings.

- *Overall fear characterized as general "dread."* A lingering fear of separation or sleeping alone. Repeated night terrors.

- *Shifts in school performance.* It's natural following trauma for children to lose concentration and for this to affect school work. When this pattern continues for months without any relief, however, even after you have worked on it with the school, you would be wise to seek help.

- *Chronic, intense anger.* Recurring tantrums. Continuing to overreact to minor situations. Frequent fights with other kids. Physical or verbal expressions of anger.

- *General lack of emotion.* In a group of children who are smiling, laughing, and seem to be enjoying themselves, if your child is staring off into space or has a blank look on his face, he may have shut down his emotions.

- *Changes in health status.* Investigate further if your child has repeated physical complaints with no detectable physical basis. For example, waking up with a stomachache every morning or reporting constant headaches. If your doctor finds no physical cause, you may want to consider counseling for the child, as the cause may be emotional stress.

- *Prolonged depression.* While it's natural that your child would feel sad, the sadness shouldn't be prolonged. Remember that kids grieve in spurts. If your child seems depressed, is often irritable, expresses feelings of worthlessness, enjoys things less, has withdrawn from friends or has changes in sleep patterns (either too much sleeping or inability to sleep) or changes in energy level (either very restless or lethargic most of the time), you should take your child to a professional. If you fear that your child is suicidal or you hear your child talk about suicide, or if your child attempts suicide, counseling is critical!

Sources of Additional Help

Grief expert Doug Manning says that the appearance of red flags doesn't automatically mean that a child needs professional help. "It may mean the child has not found a way of talking it out at home, and giving them the place and the space to do so may be all that is required. If these efforts fail and the child will not open up to you, or anyone else that you know of, then looking for some outside help is appropriate."[3]

Some places to look for help:

- *The child's natural communities.* When you feel your child needs someone other than you to talk to, consider asking an adult from one of the child's natural communities: extended family members, teachers, school counselors, pastors or youth ministers.

- *Children's grief centers.* Another ideal place to go is a center for children's grief. Most of these centers offer free support groups for children and parents who are dealing with loss. Check your yellow pages for one near you. If you don't find one, you may want to consider starting one in your community.

Steve had been dead for four years when I learned about one of the centers for children's grief in our city. I told our daughter about the Kids' Place and asked her if she would be interested in going. Katelyn jumped on it. We began to attend meetings twice a month; she went to a group with children her age and I went to the parents' group. For the first time in her life, Katelyn was with a group of kids who had all had the same experience she had—the death of a parent. During these meetings the kids talked about their experiences, made memory albums, and created memorial ornaments at Christmas. Katelyn looked forward to going each time and found her time there healing.

- *Professional help.* Should you decide your child needs professional help, do your homework. Ask people in whom you have confidence for referrals. Begin with a trusted pediatrician or family doctor. Talk to your minister. If possible, make an appointment with a therapist and discuss his or her counseling philosophy and approach to treatment to see if you agree. Check to see that the counselor is coming from a biblical perspective. Be aware that your child may not need prolonged help. It's amazing what a few visits to a good counselor can do for a family.

I began to see a Christian counselor during my husband's long recovery from his brain injury. I purposely took each of my children into a session with me to meet Pat. I wanted them to know her so that if they ever felt the need to see someone they would already have a relationship with her. After Steve's death, I went to see Pat once or twice a year for what I called a "tune-up," usually precipitated by some minor crisis with a child. Then, several years later as Katelyn began to "revisit" some of her grief, she told me she thought she needed to go talk to Pat. I was thrilled that she was willing and could even identify the need.

Elizabeth and her children also benefited from outside help after her divorce from their father. "The main thing that has helped us get through this," she says, "is our faith in Jesus Christ. I have also had an incredible Christian counselor to help me sort out my own anger as well as recognize my kids' hurts and how they express them. It has made all the difference."

One of the best things a parent can do to help grieving children is to remove the stigma from getting help. Shenae said she had to fight this feeling in herself. "You don't like to think your child needs therapy," she said. But when children are allowed this freedom, we give them a valuable life support that can keep them afloat in the roughest of waters.

Section Two

Be an Anchor

THIRTEEN

You Are Your Children's Anchor

Six weeks after the accident, Steve's medical condition stabilized, but he remained in a coma. He was moved to the rehabilitation wing of the same hospital. A team of therapists worked with him with the intent of pulling him out of the coma as well as keeping his body flexible. A month later, Steve still showed little response.

One day as I was observing Steve's therapy, the rehab psychologist called me to the conference room. As I sat across from Kathleen, something in her demeanor made me steel myself for what she was about to say: "In order to keep patients in an intense rehabilitation setting like ours, they have to meet certain goals we set for them. Because Steve is not meeting his goals, he no longer qualifies for this kind of rehab and he has to be moved to a step-down facility." She paused to let her words sink in. "This does not mean we are giving up on him. It just means Steve is not responding like we had hoped. Many times patients leave intensive rehab for a while to let their bodies continue to heal, and then return for more therapy. It's not the end, Cyndi, it's just a setback."

She looked to see if I was buying this, then continued. "The problem we're running into is that there are no appropriate sub-acute hospitals in our state. The closest facilities are in Dallas and Kansas City."

Sobs bubbled up from someplace deep inside me. It was all too much to bear. Lack of progress. Leaving rehab. Moving Steve miles away. How could this be happening? How could we do this? I wanted to jump up and run out of the hospital and keep running ... past home, past everything I knew. I wanted to run somewhere without this kind of pain and confusion. Yet I knew there was no escaping.

On the drive home, a suffocating heaviness came over me. I now had to face my ten- and six-year-old sons who thought their dad— who now lay in a coma—was next to God. How could I tell them their father was being shipped to something akin to a nursing home? I couldn't imagine my bike-riding, guitar-playing husband lying in bed between eighty- and ninety-year-old stroke victims. Unanswerable questions pelted my mind. How would our sons react to this? How would this development affect them? What did it mean for our future?

At home, the boys greeted me and then ran to play football at a neighbor's. My mom took our one-month-old baby girl from my arms and I went to my bedroom to call my friend Ramona. She and her mother had been holding a prayer group every Tuesday just to pray for Steve and our family. I wanted to give her the breaking news of the day. She wasn't home, so I left a message. My desperation and anxiety were so intense that I knew I needed to do something for myself—and do it quickly.

I could think of only two things that might help my overwhelming anxiety. One was to do something physical. The other was to focus on God's promises. I decided to do both at the same time. I found my barely used running shoes and put on a jogging suit and told my mom I was going for a run.

As my feet hit the pavement, my mind began to search for a

promise. I thought of Romans 8:28: "And we know that in all things God works for the good of those who love him, who have been called according to his purpose." I framed my situation with that verse. I didn't know how it could be true, but I believed God's Word, so it had to be true even if it didn't feel true.

Then Philippians 4:6-7 came to mind: "Don't worry about anything; instead, pray about everything; tell God your needs and don't forget to thank him for his answers. If you do this you will experience God's peace, which is far more wonderful than the human mind can understand" (LB). I slowed down to a walk to catch my breath. I began to thank God for his answers to my prayers so far. There had been many. That helped me, for a moment, to believe there would be more.

I ran all around the neighborhood, then walked, ran and walked again. The cool March air hit my face; the sunshine seemed to find my soul. My heart ached with a grief and sadness I had never known. *Steve may never wake up,* I thought. He was not responding to treatment—and he might never respond. That's what Kathleen had been hinting at when she'd told me, "We're not seeing much progress. We cannot continue this treatment with a comatose patient who is not responding." I dared to pull the curtain aside to the future and consider that Steve could remain in this state for years. In fact, he could remain in a coma for the rest of his life.

I knew that afternoon, as I wound my way back through the streets to my house, that even if Steve didn't recover *I had to survive*—not just physically, but emotionally and spiritually. My children needed me—now more than ever. I had to take care of myself so I could parent them. I was the only parent they had left, at least for now.

It's not by accident that flight attendants tell airline passengers that in an emergency they should put their air masks on first, then the child's. An adult without oxygen is no help to a child. In the same way, parents who are sinking aren't capable of keeping their children afloat. In order to help your child, you must be anchored, or you will drown in the raging waters.

This does not mean that you will never put your children first. Of course you will. Many times. But you have to find ways to nurture yourself so you can be available for your children.

This is true for you whether your family is reeling from the trauma of a death, divorce, violence, the aftermath of an accident or the diagnosis of a parent's terminal or disabling disease. While the particular circumstances may differ, the emotional, spiritual and psychological stresses of these events can threaten to drown you if you don't anchor yourself and offer your children the life preservers they will need in the upcoming months and even years.

After her divorce, Jackie had to find a balance. "I knew I had to make sacrifices for my girls," she says, "but I also knew I had to find ways to take care of myself."

While Chelle's father lay in a coma for two months, she says it was watching her mother function that gave her strength to go on. "My mom stood strong in the Lord through everything. She, with God's help, has carried the burden of raising two teenage girls and caring for a husband. I admire her and respect her because she finds her strength in God."

Writer Melinda Blau expressed it well when she said:

Granted, it is difficult to be steady in the midst of your own chaos: to exercise restraint in front of the children when you're in emotional turmoil, to be generous when you're feeling robbed, to be open when you feel like crawling into a deep, dark hole, to help your children express their feelings when you're overwhelmed by your own. But the truth is, if we want our children to come through intact, we don't have a choice.[1]

Of course, my problems were still there when I came back home from my run that day. I still felt like a ton of bricks had been dumped in my heart. But I also felt more capable of dealing with our situation. I knew I could make it through the night, and that's all I needed. That's all any of us need ... the resources to make it through one more night, one more day. The good news is we don't have to do it alone. God will help us find our anchor in him so we can hold strong for the children in our life.

FOURTEEN

Anchor Yourself in Christ

I don't know how people get through crises without faith," Jackie told me. "You have to have a sense of higher calling that only faith can bring. It brings a rest and peace in the storm. Sometimes God calms the storm; sometimes he calms the child; sometimes he lets the storm rage and you only have your faith in him to hold on to."

Our faith is one of the strongest anchors we have. It provides strength when we are exhausted, support when we are alone, peace for questions without answers, healing for our pain. It anchors us in the rock when we are floundering. Without it we are subject to the winds and torrents of our circumstances and emotions.

Staying in God's Word

"After my husband died, I came up with a plan of action," says Deb, mother of four. "I chose a particular chair in my bedroom and promised myself that when I felt overwhelmed, I would sit in that chair and open my Bible to the book of Psalms, and I'd stay there until I got some relief. It helped a lot."

After her husband left her, Paula found herself needing God in a new way. Now, twenty years later, she has two grown daughters, both married to Christian men and establishing Christian homes. "I believe my daughters are stronger emotionally and spiritually than they might have been," she says. "Right after the divorce I read my Bible constantly. The girls saw that. It modeled a way of life for them, which they now imitate. I know they have scars, but I also know this is one area in our lives that is stronger because of what we went through."

Both of these women found that the way to anchor themselves in the stormy aftermath of death and divorce was to focus on God by staying in his Word. You can too. Read the Psalms. Personalize them. Memorize God's promises. Quote them as you go about your day, as you wake in the morning, as you lie down at night.

Paula says that along with making a conscious decision to focus on God, she also made a deliberate choice not to focus on finding a mate. "I just figured that if I trusted God to take care of us, then I could leave even that in his hands." Jackie concurs. "I had so many friends who seemed desperate to find someone. That didn't seem like the right approach. So I've tried to leave that matter with God."

Lisa sums up this perspective when she says, "I remember walking through my single life feeling I was completely content to stay where I was because first of all I had established a relationship with Jesus. He was my man! I had developed a love I had never known before. In my mind nobody could satisfy me more than Jesus."

Journaling

Many women report that journaling has been a lifesaver for them as they've struggled to move ahead after a tragedy or devastating event in their lives. Elizabeth cites her journal, next to her relationship with Christ, as being her biggest help in her ability to heal: "My journal is such a release for me. I feel like I can tell God just exactly how bad I hurt or how excited I am about his grace in my life! I love to go back and see where he has brought me."

Paula, too, credits journaling with helping her keep her emotional and spiritual balance. She first used it as a way to keep track of her prayer requests and answers. Then one day God nudged her to write down a list of praises. She says this was a turning point in her healing as her journaling helped her begin to focus on the good instead of on the pain and loss.

Even if you have never been successful at journaling in the past, you might find it a valuable outlet during a time of crisis or loss. For one thing, you never have to worry about talking too much or saying the same thing over and over again. You are free to be completely honest—to dump on the page without fear of how your words might be received.

Try it for a week or two and see if you find relief. You don't need to purchase an expensive book—a spiral notebook will do. It can be lined or unlined, depending on your preference. What matters is that you write down your thoughts in one place rather than on pieces of paper here and there. Date each of your entries, including the year. Years down the road you may not remember exactly when you wrote each entry.

Some additional ideas for using your journal:

- During your quiet times each day, write out Scripture verses that encourage you. Include why the verses are meaningful to you.
- Write out your prayers to God.
- List your prayer requests in one column, including the date you first begin to pray for this request. In the opposite column you can write God's answer to your prayer and the date it was answered. This can provide a documented history of God's work in your life.
- Record the day's events and how you felt about them.

Regardless of what you use or how you use it, try journaling. It may be an avenue of release and renewal in your life.

Praise Songs

Music can help us focus on God and nurture our own souls. Ami says that when she tried to sing herself she would always end up crying. Instead, she played music to enrich and lift her spirit.

Music encouraged me as well. As our family waited to see if my husband would emerge from his coma, music became a way for me to nurture my faith.

One day as I stepped into the warm water of the shower, the weight of our lives felt like a heavy ball attached to my heart. A thought popped up. *Sing.*

"What?" I questioned.

It came again: *Sing.*

A praise chorus came to mind. I shampooed my hair and scrubbed my skin, all the while singing my song. Not because I felt like it, but because I knew the words of the song were true. Because I knew—despite the circumstances—that God loved me, loved Steve and loved my kids. Singing helped me remember that. It helped me focus on the Lord, not on the pain. Music gave flight to my spirit above the sorrows of this earth.

As I toweled off, I realized the person who'd come out of the shower was different from the person who'd gone in. Oh, the ache in my soul remained; there was no washing it away. But I had a stronger sense of God's presence, comfort and control.

God Meets Us in Unplanned Moments

Perhaps never in your life are the demands so great as when you are going through a family crisis. Don't be fooled into thinking you can't nurture your faith if you don't have huge blocks of time to spend praying or reading God's Word. God can meet with you in unplanned and unexpected moments. You can focus your thoughts on God, even in the midst of a harried schedule:

- Keep a small Bible or inspirational book in your purse or car. Read it while you wait at the doctor's office or hairdresser or hospital.
- Borrow or purchase good tapes and CD's to listen to in the car as you run errands or go back and forth to the hospital or work. These can be music or books and speakers on tape.
- Keep your journal with you so you can jot down prayers and thoughts when you have a moment.

Do what you can to feed your faith. It is the most important anchor you have.

FIFTEEN

Take Care of Yourself

During the months that Steve lay in a coma, swells of sadness would rise up in me. I had heard that when you feel that kind of pain, the best remedy is to lean into it, experience it. So I tried it. This is part of what therapists call *processing the grief*. We want to run away from it or push it back down inside us, but the first step in healing is to acknowledge, even name the emotion, and then feel it.

"Grief is not an enemy to be avoided. Grief is a process that leads to healing. It is like peeling an onion; it comes off one layer at a time and you cry a lot."[1] One of the best things we can do for ourselves (and ultimately for our children) is to grieve. If we ignore or fight our pain, it will not go away. The only way to get past these emotions is to feel them.

- Let yourself cry.
- Find someone to talk to; let them know you need an ear, not advice.
- Get a pillow and punch it.
- Journal your thoughts and feelings.[2]

In addition, learn what you can about the grief process. Read books on grief. Search the Internet. The more you know about what you can expect to feel, the less you will be surprised by your reactions.

Give yourself time. The closer we are to the loss, the more intense our emotions.

Most people come through a catastrophe and wonder, *Will this pain ever go away?* Just know that it will. Be good to yourself; allow yourself permission to grieve for as long as you need to.

Be Authentic

Deb was afraid to show her sadness to her children. Now she realizes this was a mistake. "Where I went wrong was I didn't show emotion to the family. I felt I needed to keep it all together for them and would take care of myself in private. What I didn't realize was that they all felt I didn't miss Dad. Boy, were they wrong!"

It's okay for your kids to see you cry once in a while. If they do, talk with them about why you are crying. Tell them, "I feel sad today and I feel like crying." If your children ask if you're okay, say, "No, I'm not okay, but I will be. I can handle this and will be able to take care of myself." When your kids see you get up and go on about your day, they learn that the intensity of grief passes when we express it and that we can move on and go about our lives—until the next time.

Authentic mourning is applicable in whatever circumstances you find yourself, not just after a death. For instance, if you admit your sorrow over a divorce it will help your children deal with their own feelings of loss. Even if you initiated the divorce, you will still have a sense of sadness for your children and your dreams.

While it is okay for children to see you cry, it is not good for them to see you repeatedly fall apart. If your emotions get too strong and out of control, you might overwhelm them. Take note of how you are doing.

Are You Moving Through Your Grief?

Are you processing your grief? Are you moving through it? If months have passed and you do not feel any lessening of your grief, you might need to find someone to talk to who is knowledgeable about grief and loss.

Review the list below. Experts suggest that if you experience five or more of these symptoms for longer than two weeks, or if any of them are interfering with your daily routine, you may need to see your doctor or a professional.

- A persistent sad, anxious or "empty" mood
- Sleeping too little or too much
- Reduced/increased appetite and weight loss or gain
- Restlessness or irritability
- Persistent physical symptoms that don't respond to treatment
- Difficulty concentrating, remembering or making decisions
- Fatigue or loss of energy
- Feeling guilty, hopeless or worthless
- Thoughts of death or suicide

Remember that you are a model for your kids. They will do what they see you doing. You don't have to be a stoic; you need to be real. Let your kids observe you grieving in a healthy way. If this is not happening, get some help—for your sake and theirs.

Don't Try to Do It All

Bill, a widower left with a fifteen-year-old daughter, says he probably did too much and expected too little of Krista. "I worked full time, took care of the house and made home-cooked meals most nights. In retrospect, I could have called on her to do more."

Give yourself time to rest by delegating chores around the house that your kids can help you tackle. Call a family meeting to discuss how everyone can pitch in. Children are generally more willing to help when they have a voice in the plans.

Once Steve came home from the hospital, I taught my boys, who were ten and fourteen at the time, to do their own laundry. It was a chore they easily managed and it was a big help to me.

One widowed father kept a notebook on the kitchen counter with a page for each necessary chore, such as unloading the dishwasher and taking out the trash. Under each job he listed each family member's name, one after another until he filled up the page. When a child completed the chore, he crossed out his name and the next person knew it was his turn.

Remember, when you enlist your children's help, give up your perfectionism. While it's important that children learn to do a job right, they may not do it perfectly to your adult ideals. That's okay.

As with other things, finding the right balance is the key. Children are just that—children—and you don't want to overburden them with too many household chores. Avoid turning them into your miniature maids. On the other hand, don't be afraid to ask for extra help. Once when I was venting at how overwhelmed I was by all the demands on my time, my twelve-year-old son said, "Mom, we'd help if you just told us what to do. Don't expect us to like it, but we'll do it."

Once you decide to let some things go, don't beat yourself up because you can't do everything or be everything. No one can. That kind of guilt robs you of the energy you need for the things you *can* do.

Reduce Your Stress Level

As you continue to work through your grief, take steps to reduce the stress in your life. Most people have trouble concentrating following traumatic events. To help you keep track of responsibilities, write them down. The less you have to mentally juggle the better off you will be.

Take a hard look at your schedule, your children's schedule and your life in general. What absolutely has to be done? You may have to keep that doctor's appointment, but do you have to hit the half-price sale at the mall? Take some pressure off yourself and your children and ask God for wisdom as you truly weed out the don't have-to's from the have-to's. Let some things go. For every day that you make it through, remember to reward yourself ... with a walk with a friend, a pat on the back, a long, hot bath.

And try to keep a sense of humor. Once the nurses in the critical care unit realized Steve's visitors were going to be frequent and numerous, they gave us our own private waiting room. Sometimes the room would erupt with laughter as family and friends told "Steve stories." I remember thinking no one would ever believe the tragedy we were dealing with if they walked by and heard us. But it was a great source of comfort to have moments of levity amidst such heartache.

As I traveled the fifteen-minute drive back and forth to the hospital each day, I often played speaking tapes by Patsy Clairmont that a friend had sent to me. They were hilarious. I would throw my head back and cackle as she described her antics. It was a brief reprieve from the heavy load I was carrying most other times.

Give yourself permission to laugh. Allow yourself to keep a sense of humor. It will be one additional way to keep yourself afloat.

SIXTEEN

Let Go of Anger and Resentment

A nger is a natural response when we are hurt or afraid.

When Fred was killed on his way home from a short-term mission trip in Mexico, Ami felt angry with God. Why would God let this happen to Fred when Fred had taken his own vacation time to serve as a missionary? Ami wanted an apology from God, and she wanted him to acknowledge how tough Fred's loss was for her and her three young children.

When Gary learned that his ex-wife, Liz, had hit and physically abused their sons, he was angry. How could she have harmed her own kids—particularly when she knew the pain and suffering it caused because she had been victimized in similar ways by her own mother? Gary was angry because Liz had constantly refused to get help throughout their marriage. Rather than going to a counselor to work on the problems in their marriage, she chose to divorce him. He was also angry at the system because even after involving child services in the situation, a judge had ruled that Liz still had custodial rights with their youngest son. (The oldest, at sixteen, refused to visit his mother because of the physical abuse.)

While it's okay to feel anger, it's not okay to hang on to it. We must find a way to let it go. Most experts agree that parental anger does more to damage children than death or divorce. "How well you handle the divorce transition and your own anger will affect your children far more than the divorce itself."[1] That's a sobering thought.

Dr. Archibald Hart, a Christian professor of psychology and author of *Helping Children Survive Divorce*, concurs. "Getting rid of your resentment is crucial to the well-being of your children," he says. He feels strongly that "all feelings of resentment must be resolved as soon as possible after a divorce if any good is to come of it. There is no excuse for anyone here."[2]

Letting go of anger is one of the biggest challenges a wounded parent can face. Many people complain about an ex-spouse's anger, but fail to deal with their own. Dr. Hart recommends four steps to take to defuse anger and resentment: develop a holy perspective on your hurts, dispose of your need for revenge, declare your forgiving spirit to those who have hurt you and deliberately turn your resentment into kindness.

Develop a Holy Perspective on Your Hurts

When we realize how much our own sin has hurt God, it helps us keep the hurt others have inflicted on us in perspective. We can never forgive someone else more than God has forgiven us. Understanding this may be a process, not a one-time event. But as you pray and ask God to help you see your own fallenness, he will develop a new perspective on your hurt.

Dispose of Your Need for Revenge

How do we do this? By forgiving those who have hurt us. This means giving up our right to retaliate even when we have every right to be angry and resentful, even when we are victims. This is for our sake, not for the sake of the one who has hurt us.

Paula's experience after her husband walked out illustrates this point. "One day as I leaned over the oven," she says, "the Lord's presence came right up beside me and in a gentle voice God said, 'You know, Paula, you are going to have to forgive.' 'I know,' I replied, 'but I can't just yet.' I knew it would take a divine touch for me to be able to forgive because I was not capable of doing it myself."

Paula rightfully understood that a holy God required forgiveness, but she also knew a loving God would patiently work with her as she came to that point. She goes on to say, "Eighteen to twenty months passed as I continued to experience God's healing in my heart. Then one day, I knew the time had come. I knelt by the loveseat in my bedroom and forgave my ex. An interesting thing began to happen within days of that experience. My finances began to improve, my shattered self-concept and self-worth began to return, and my depression was replaced with joy and hope. Month after month, God began to bring new blessings and healing into my life."

Declare Your Forgiving Spirit to Those Who Have Hurt You

Dr. Hart says the next step is communicating to the person who has hurt you or continues to hurt you that "you will not allow their actions to make you bitter. You will not retaliate or take revenge." Rather than encouraging the forgiven person to continue to hurt you, this commonly causes him or her to stop. If someone does persist in hurting you, Dr. Hart suggests that you ask whoever it is to stop doing it, to be "lovingly assertive and honestly confrontive."[3]

Deliberately Turn Your Resentment Into Kindness

The final step of forgiveness is acting on your new position. You must now behave as the person you would like to be. Eventually, you will become that person.

Jackie felt that God offered her just such a challenge the Christmas after her divorce. Due to Frank's mental health problems, he had been unable to hold a job. When Jackie received her Christmas bonus from her teaching job, she started to put the check in her purse and sensed God saying to her, "That is not your money. I want you to give it to Frank." Jackie argued with God about this for a while, reminding him that she was the one shouldering all the responsibility for the children. She continued to sense God urging her to give the money to Frank. "It became so much not my money that I knew it would be a sin to keep it," she says. So, without fully understanding, she obeyed.

Sometimes we have to do things that don't come naturally .... until we do them. The more we act like the person we truly want to be, the person God has in mind for us to be, the more natural it becomes. Here are some things you can do to cooperate with God in changing your behavior:

1. Notice negative patterns in your behavior, especially as they relate to your ex-spouse. Ask God to help you become aware of them and to check your spirit when they "raise their ugly heads."

2. Take responsibility for your own behavior. Know you are the only one you can control. Stop blaming.

3. Decide how you will act, and act the way you would like. Ask God to empower you to be the mature, healthy person you want to be and your child needs you to be.

Forgiveness is a difficult but essential process. You can't be a true anchor for your children if you harbor rage and resentment. The best news is you do not have to do it alone. God will work with you as you move toward forgiveness. He's done it for Paula and Jackie. He'll do it for you.

Ten Do's for Your Relationship With Your Ex

1. Make a conscious choice to see your ex not as your ex-spouse but as a co-parent, much like a business partner. Your business is co-parenting your children.

2. Acknowledge that your children need the other parent and that the other parent has something to give.

3. Find something about your ex that you can respect. Try to see your ex through your child's eyes.

4. Avoid talking negatively about the other parent in front of your child—do not call names or blame the other parent for problems. When you attack your child's other parent, she feels as if you are attacking her.

5. Encourage the other parent's involvement in the child's life: visitation, school and other activities. Children who are deprived of contact with the other parent tend to idealize the lost parent.

6. Talk directly to the other parent—not through your children.

7. Do not drill your child about what is going on in the other parent's home.

8. Do not argue in front of the children. Be courteous. Keep your emotions in control. If you cannot, then end the conversation until you can. "It's not their parents' divorce that upsets children; it's the ongoing conflict that threatens their world and diminishes their self-esteem."[4]

9. Do not discuss financial and legal issues when the children are present.

10. Do not wait for the other parent to come around. You do the right thing. Healing always begins with yourself.

Thoughts on Anger

Be quick to listen, slow to speak and slow to become angry.

JAMES 1:19

- Anger and hostility show you are still strongly attached to a person. The opposite of love is not hate, but detachment.

- Don't react to your ex-partner. Reacting means your ex has control over you. Instead, respond. Responding means you are in charge. Think before replying.

- Remember—some things should never be said.

SEVENTEEN

Get a Support Network

Before my husband's accident I saw myself as someone who was capable of receiving from others—but I always wanted to reciprocate so that I could feel like I was doing my fair share. For example, friends and I would often exchange babysitting. Whatever the favor was, I tried to make sure I always returned it.

Early one morning after talking with the neurosurgeon, I realized that Steve's recovery was going to be a long process. As I thought about what the doctor had said, I felt a nudge from God: "If you are going to make it through this, you are going to have to let other people help you. You are not going to make it alone. And you are not going to be able to keep score."

Little did I know what that would entail. In the months that followed, I looked back on that moment in the waiting room with thanksgiving. God had prepared me to receive all that others would give me. We needed much more than I possibly could have given back.

If you feel this way, you aren't alone. Jackie told me, "I had to fight the feeling that I could do this on my own because deep down I knew that I couldn't, and that it wouldn't be in my girls' best interest. But there is a strong cultural pull to go that way." Debbie says if she had one thing to do over, she would accept more help. "People offered to help, but I hated to take them up on it. Looking back, I wish I had been more willing."

Accepting Practical Help

I remember the first time I went over to our friend Mark's house armed with my phone book-sized stack of medical bills. He and I spent the evening trying to sort through what had been paid, needed to be paid or could wait. I left with a headache and a grateful heart for an insurance-agent friend who understood insurance forms.

If your family has been hit with tragedy, let others help you. People who care for you often feel helpless in the face of a crisis. Allowing them to pitch in with practical support helps them put legs to their love. More importantly, it helps your children by taking care of needs you may not be able to handle, and it allows them to see love in action. Do not be hesitant to take others up on their offers to

- Cook meals
- Clean your house
- Baby-sit
- Go to the grocery store for you
- Drive your kids to activities and events
- Help with yard work
- Make small repairs around the house

Above all else, be gracious and thank them. Know that someday when you are in a different place, you will gladly bless someone else in the same way you have been blessed.

Build a Support Network

When I learned that Steve wasn't responding to treatment, I went home and called my prayer group. I needed to talk to people who cared about me. I needed their prayers. One of the best ways you can anchor yourself is to stay in touch with friends and family who are supportive. Do not isolate yourself.

I've talked with many single parents who agree that a support system can really make the difference in our ability to be an anchor for our kids. Jackie says, "I was blessed with a support system. It's crucial to have a faith community that prays for us and lets us be who we are. Even when I knew I had to walk through it alone, I had people who cared about me." Elizabeth agrees: "My family, church, friends have been unbelievable. I have one friend in particular who has checked on me daily and in the beginning, three or four times a day."

Bill's pastor offered him this kind of support when his wife died. "He really helped me man-to-man," Bill recalls. "He was a spiritual sounding board. He let me vent, let me ask questions. Being a guy, at times he wanted to fix it for me. I told him all he had to do was be there—and he was."

Single parents, especially, need support. We have God, but sometimes we need him to come to us wearing clothes and with a warm hand to hold. People need people; we're made that way. Especially in difficult days, the body of Christ really does need each other. Identify your support people and use them.

The church is the first place to find such support. Through Sunday school classes, Bible studies and other small groups, people develop friendships that are with them in the good times and in the bad.

You also might want to join a support group. Many churches now offer groups designed to specifically address various needs—divorce recovery groups, grief workshops, single parent groups. If you are dealing with serious illness, injury or death, check your local hospitals and medical affiliates. Many offer support groups for people whose loved ones have been disabled because of a stroke or brain injury or who are fighting cancer or other life-threatening illnesses. Hospice and funeral homes also offer grief groups.

Be careful that the people you depend on are supportive. Some relationships may need to be put on hold. Everyone may not be able to handle your grief and sorrow. Others may be consistently negative, critical or pessimistic. If this is true for some of your friends or family, you may have to limit your contact with them for a while. This is okay—and necessary. When we are trying to keep our kids afloat we must avoid situations and people that pull us under.

See a Counselor

Many people find real help with a solid, biblical counselor. A wise counselor will be a great listener and sounding board who can help you identify trouble spots and advise you in overcoming them. A counselor can guide you in understanding your reactions and responses and can help you know you are "normal" (or not!).

This is not a time in your life to be a Lone Ranger Christian. You need the love and support of others as you attempt to love and support your children. To be an anchor, find a friend, group or counselor who can support you in this very important role.

EIGHTEEN

Pray!

Jackie had watched her husband's mind gradually deteriorate. Frank had gone from doctor to doctor, yet his behavior became increasingly bizarre. He lost jobs, refused to take medication and developed paranoia. For her daughters' sakes, she needed out of the marriage. Jackie knew she must have custody of the girls, but Frank saw this as her attempt to take them completely away from him. With the testimony of doctors, psychologists and friends, she knew she could win her case in court, but she preferred not to drag everyone through that. Instead she decided to pray. Who knew what God would do?

Weeks later, one evening around 10:00 P.M., Frank called Jackie. A few days earlier his car had been stolen and he was now phoning to tell her that the police had located it. Frank asked if she would drive him to the scene. Even though she was tired after a long day, Jackie agreed. When Frank got into his car to leave, it would not start. Jackie stayed until it finally started and then followed Frank home.

She was about to drive off when Frank called to her. "I knew by the tone of his voice that something was different," she says. "I knew what he was going to say." Frank told her he would no longer fight her for custody of the girls. He would agree for her to have sole custody.

God answered Jackie's prayer. He also graciously answered Debbie's prayer for guidance. For months Debbie had been praying about her home situation. Her husband's drug and alcohol abuse was increasing. They had four children under eleven years old and she was growing more concerned for their safety and hers. Yet she wasn't sure how she would make it as a single parent with only a part-time job. She didn't want to move her children out of the frying pan and into the fire. So she simply began to ask, "God, give me a sign."

One afternoon she ran to the grocery store. Upon returning home, she found her street full of police cars. Terrified that the police were arresting her husband and might be taking her children, she rushed into the house. To her surprise, the officers were answering a call next door. Debbie said that as relief flooded through her, she realized this was her sign, an answer to her prayer about what to do: *get out now.*

She immediately implemented the plan she had been developing. While work on the church's crisis house was being completed, family friends offered temporary housing in their home for Debbie and her four children. Once the crisis home had been remodeled, they moved in.

While this was only the beginning of the challenges she faced, God gave Debbie the direction she asked for and then gave her the strength to follow through.

Prayer is an anchor that goes deep ... all the way to the heart of God. No doubt there will be times you do not feel like praying. That's okay. Pray anyway. You will be angry. Confused. Scared. Pray!

Most likely you will not have hours to spend in prayer, so pray throughout your day. In the car on the way to school or work. As you do dishes and the kids run outside for ten minutes. You don't have to be on your knees or in a closet. God is your heavenly Father. He hurts when you hurt, just as you do with your own children. Turn to him with your pain and confusion. Talk to him and allow him to talk to you.

Praise God for Who He Is

Begin by focusing on who God is. You might make a list of the names of God that can be found in Scripture:

- Jehovah-jireh—The Lord will provide. "And my God will meet all your needs according to his glorious riches in Christ Jesus" (Phil 4:19).
- El Roi—The God who sees. "For a man's ways are in full view of the Lord, and he examines all his paths" (Prv 5:21).
- Jehovah-rapha—The Lord who heals. "He heals the broken-hearted and binds up their wounds" (Ps 147:3).
- Jehovah-shammah—The Lord is there. "Where can I go from your Spirit? Where can I flee from your presence? If I go up to the heavens, you are there; if I make my bed in the depths, you are there. If I rise on the wings of the dawn, if I settle on the far side of the sea, even there your hand will guide me, your right hand will hold me fast" (Ps 139:7-10).
- Jehovah-shalom—The Lord is peace. "Do not be anxious about anything, but in everything, by prayer and petition, with thanksgiving, present your request to God. And the peace of God, which transcends all understanding, will guard your hearts and your minds in Christ Jesus" (Phil 4:6-7).

Select one name a day or one a week and praise God for that aspect of his character. Then apply that attribute to your situation. Look for examples of how God has shown himself to you in that way. Ask him to reveal that aspect of his character to you. For example, Philippians 4:19 promises that God will provide for all our needs. What does that mean for you in your present circumstances? Allow him to bring examples to your mind of times he has provided, and let your faith build on that.

Consider identifying a daily routine during which you can focus on praising God—when you are taking a shower or brushing your teeth, for example. Ask God to remind you to praise him each time you perform that activity. Eventually it will become a habit.

Thank God for His Grace

Focusing on what God has done for us helps us deal with life's difficulties. We can thank him for many things, particularly the people he has placed in our lives and the things he has done for us.

Thank him for all the people who are actively helping you. One day I had a particularly stressful morning getting the boys off to school. We woke up late, ten-month old Katelyn was fussy, the boys' shoes were nowhere to be found and a therapist from Steve's hospital had called to reschedule a meeting for that morning. I pulled up to the drop-off point for car riders at Lake Park Elementary later than usual. Jeremy and Tate ran in with a note I had scratched out on back of a pizza coupon, explaining why they were tardy. I couldn't go in myself since I was still dressed in my robe and slippers. By now, Katelyn's frustration level was as high as mine was, and she was screaming and flailing to get out of her car seat.

As I turned the car around the circle drive to head home, I began to cry. "God, I can't do this anymore. I'm so tired. I can't do this alone." The words had no more than slipped from my tongue when I sensed God's presence with me in that chaotic van. And his still small voice said to me, "Cyndi, you're not alone. If ever anyone has gone through a crisis and had help and support and love, it has been you."

I began to think of all the people who had shown their love to me and Steve and my kids: My sister and brother-in-law had made frequent trips from out of town to help around the house, buy groceries and take us all out to dinner. My mom had literally packed up her apartment and moved in with me to be my temporary "wife." Steve's mom and step-dad kept opposite vigils from me at the hospital so that I had time to be with my children at night. They also offered generous financial help. Friends like Susan, Kathy, Laronda, Bettie Lou and many others had come to the hospital with me for months so that I did not have to be alone. Dads like Mark, Terry, Ron, Mike and Bill looked out for my sons as if they were their own. I had not been alone. God had surrounded me with a multitude of loving hands and hearts to help me bear this tremendous load.

By the time I got home, Katelyn was still screaming, the phone was ringing again and the early morning whirlwind called breakfast that had torn through the kitchen still needed to be cleaned up. But I was refreshed and ready to tackle the day's troubles. On my way home God had met me. He had gently reminded me of all the people he had placed in my life in the midst of our pain. I was not alone, and I knew it.

Thank him for what he has done for you. Steve used to teach a Sunday school lesson entitled "Life Isn't Fair—Thank God." He had written it out of his frustration as a father hearing our kids protest, "That's not fair!" In this lesson, Steve used Scripture to show that all of us deserve God's judgment and punishment because of our sinfulness. But because of his enormous mercy and love, God sent Jesus to take our place. So it's true that life isn't fair. We don't get what we really deserve—and we need to thank God for that. Ask God to help you realize this truth and believe it. When we allow him to help us comprehend what he did for us, gratitude begins to fill our hearts.

God wants to hear from you. He longs to meet your needs. Bring them to him. But if your prayer life consists only of a list, you'll be missing much of what he has for you. When we are hurting, it's tempting to bring him only our pain. Allow him to turn your eyes off of yourself and onto him.

Pray the Scriptures

Find a scripture that describes God as you need him now and pray that verse back to him. For example, Psalm 68:5 says, "A father to the fatherless, a defender of widows, is God in his holy dwelling." You might pray: "Oh God, you are a father to the fatherless, a defender of widows. Be that to me, Father. Be that to my children. Be a father to my children when they have none. Protect them and provide for them as a father would. Help them to feel your love as truly as they would feel the love of a physical father holding them in his lap. Be my defender against the enemy who wants to beat me down, discourage me, rob me of peace and joy. Please defend me against worry and anxiety. Help me to remember that YOU ARE

GOD and you are on my side. Amen."

I like praying the Psalms. You might want to look up different versions until you find the wording that says it best for you. Then adapt it:

- Write it out.
- Personalize it, inserting your name.
- Pray it back to God.
- Ask God to teach you that it's true for you.
- Memorize it.
- Put it on a 3x5 card and place it where you'll see it.
- Share it with your children.

At one point I was experiencing some tremendous fears about my future. My anxiety was keeping me from sleeping. God directed me to Psalm 34 in *The Message*. "Is anyone crying for help? God is listening, ready to rescue you. If your heart is broken, you'll find God right there; if you're kicked in the gut, he'll help you catch your breath" (Ps 34:17-18). I spent days in that chapter, journaling it, praying it. Eventually my fears subsided as I prayed God's Word over myself and my family.

Pray for Your Children

While Steve was in the hospital, I spent hours waiting in the CCU and I spent a lot of time praying. It was in the midst of my prayer that God nudged me to go home and play New Year's Eve games with my sons and, more importantly, charged me to continue to be there for them. During those times when I was telling God I felt depressed or overwhelmed, I sensed him showing me my need to let others help me and opening up my spirit to receive that help.

In the quiet of the waiting room, two prayers formed in my heart. "Lord, please make Steve's life count"—which is what Steve really cared about. The other was, "God, use this for good in the life of my children."

I saw God begin to answer this in one way a few months after Steve's wreck. Jeremy asked me about our income and how we were getting money while his dad was in the hospital and I was not working. I told him we had a little savings, that Steve's radio station and clients had held fundraisers, and that our church had set up a fund for people to give to our family. I could see him taking this all in.

Then, very seriously, my ten-year-old said to me, "Mom, do you know what this tells me?"

"What's that, Jer?" I asked.

"It tells me that I should live my life just like my dad so that if anything bad ever happens to me, people will want to help my family, too."

I was speechless. There were lots of things Jeremy could be feeling and thinking since a drunk driver had hit his dad. But on this day, he was seeing God at work and being drawn to a life that God honors. I could not ask for more.

You're reading this book because you love and care about your children. So does God. His plan is to "prosper [them], and not to harm [them]" (Jer 29:11). We may not know all that entails, but we can be assured that God loves our children more than we do. He cares even more about their outcome. If you have trouble believing that, then that's where you start: "God, teach me that you love my children even more than I do."

As we ask God to use this loss for good in the lives of our children, there are some specific ways we can pray:

- *That God will be a father to them.* "A father to the fatherless, a defender of widows, is God in his holy dwelling" (Ps 68:5).

- *That God will protect his purpose in their lives.* "For I know the plans I have for you," declares the Lord, "plans to prosper you and not to harm you, plans to give you hope and a future" (Jer 29:11).

- *That God will teach our children that he loves them.* "We need have no fear of someone who loves us perfectly; his perfect love for us eliminates all dread of what he might do to us. If we are afraid, it is for fear of what he might do to us, and shows that we are not fully convinced that he really loves us" (1 Jn 4:18, LB).

- *That God will heal their brokenness.* "He heals the brokenhearted and binds up their wounds" (Ps 147:3).

- *That God will use this experience to draw them to him, not away from him.* "But I, when I am lifted up from the earth, will draw all men to myself" (Jn 12:32).

- *That God will send people into our children's lives to make up for the loss.* "I will repay you for the years the locusts have eaten" (Jl 2:25).

- *That God will help us as parents to be sensitive to whatever our kids need from us.* "He tends his flock like a shepherd: He gathers the lambs in his arms and carries them close to his heart; he gently leads those that have young" (Is 40:11).

Ami was concerned about her ten-year-old daughter, Amanda, whose neck had been broken in the accident that had killed her father. Ami prayed fervently for Amanda's physical healing, but it was her emotional needs that concerned Ami the most. Ami began to ask God to protect Amanda from nightmares after such a traumatic event. To everyone's amazement, Amanda never had a nightmare. Ami knows God intervened to protect Amanda from further pain.

Praying for Your Former Spouse

When Jill's husband told her and their twin sons that he wanted a divorce, she immediately started praying for him. "The next morning as I sat at the breakfast table with our boys, I asked them if they would promise to pray for each other and for their dad. In the months that followed, I discovered that you cannot despise someone you are praying for. When I was tempted to feel bitter, I would pray for deeper love."

You may not be able to pray for your former spouse just yet, but don't hesitate to ask God to help you want to. Praying for those who have hurt us can do us a world of good. Jill's sons are nineteen years old now. "My boys are growing up to be godly young men with hearts full of compassion," Jill says. "God taught the boys how to love without reserve, even when it hurts." God was able to teach them this because they had a mother who prayed ... for them and for their father.

Pray for Yourself

And while you're praying, don't forget to pray for yourself. Jackie said she certainly felt the need to pray more for herself after her divorce and as she became a single parent. I like Jackie's prayer:

God, give me the knowledge and information I need in each situation, wisdom to know what to do with it and strength to carry it out. Amen.

That's a prayer we can all pray, regardless of our family's state.

Pray your praise! Pray your anguish. Pray for your children and for yourself. Pray when you can and where you can! Pray like Elizabeth, who says, "I feel like I can tell God just exactly how bad I hurt or how excited I am about his grace in my life. I love to go back and see where he has brought me. It is neat to see all of the answered prayers." Keep that two-way line of communication open and it will be a support that lasts for a lifetime.

NINETEEN

An Attitude of Gratitude

The morning after I gave birth to Katelyn, a volunteer tapped on my door and tiptoed in with a floral delivery. I forced my eyes open and delicately tried to turn my sore body to get a better look at the arrangement. I was stunned. Sitting on my window ledge were a dozen of the most gorgeous roses I had ever seen. The sun peeked through my blinds, bathing the blooms in light. They took my breath away. Pink and perfect, they were surrounded by fans of ferns.

I had never seen flowers so beautiful. The aide handed me an envelope. I opened it. Beneath the kind note was the signature of a person I had never met but whom I recognized as one of Steve's clients at the radio station.

Wow, what a generous gift from someone I don't even know, I thought. Then my eyes began to fill with tears and a sorrow came over me, turning the moment from one of delight to self-pity. The flowers were lovely, but they were not from my husband. Steve had brought me roses at the births of my other two children. Not only wasn't he present at Katelyn's birth, he had no idea she'd even been born. He still lay in a coma in the rehab unit three floors above my room. I fell back onto my pillow, the pain in my heart greater than the pain from my stitches.

I sobbed at the sadness of it all. I cried for my baby girl who had missed her father's presence at her birth. I cried for my two sons who had paced the floor in their daddy's place last night as I labored. But mostly I cried for myself.

Then, God came quietly alongside me in room 227 and whispered, "There are always two handles."

I knew what he meant. Years earlier Steve and I had heard our friend Richard Angell preach a sermon on learning to view life from more than one perspective. This pastor painted a word picture of a pot with two handles and taught us that there were always at least two "handles" to pick up any of the circumstances in our lives. Moreover, we had control over which handle we used. Richard reminded us that we were the ones who decided how we were going to see our circumstances.

This lesson stuck with both of us. Later, as Steve and I would catch each other complaining or whining, we'd chide, "What handle are you picking this up with?"

Now God whispered, "Could it be that when Steve was unable to send you flowers, I provided them for you? Not only did I provide them, I sent you the most spectacular display of roses you've ever seen. They can be a reminder of what you've lost. Or they can be a reminder of what you still have—a heavenly Father who loves and cares for you."

I cried again—this time out of gratitude for such a personal God who knew just what kind of special delivery to send my way.

Finding the Good Amid the Bad

When we are in the midst of difficult circumstances, it is not easy to see past our pain and loss. Cultivating an attitude of gratitude does not mean that we pretend nothing is wrong. It means that we allow God to help us find the good that still exists in our lives and thank him for it. This honors God and helps us.

Cultivating an attitude of gratitude is a conscious decision. 1 Thessalonians 1:18 tells us to "give thanks in all circumstances." This does not mean we thank God for the sin and evil in the world. God did not expect me to thank him that a drunken nineteen-year-old illegally drove and smashed into my husband's car, changing our life forever. But I could thank him that a cardiologist and medic-flight nurse were passing the scene immediately after it happened and worked with Steve until an ambulance got there.

I could thank God that Steve's radio station, KTOK, had excellent medical insurance and took care of every need he had. I could thank him for family and friends who rallied around our family for months to support us.

God does not expect you to praise him for the affair that broke up your marriage or the cancer that is destroying your mate's body. But we can, and must, find things to be thankful for despite our circumstances.

No one was a better example to me of this truth than was Steve himself.

After emerging from his coma only to battle countless physical complications, Steve went through a terrible depression. He wanted to see no one but the kids and me.

Fifteen months after the accident, spring returned to Oklahoma and we started seeing signs of the "old Steve." The warm days and sunshine seemed to breathe a new spirit into him. Everyone noticed. His sense of humor returned. For the first time, he began to ask me about something besides his children. He would question me about things at church, our friends and family. I was encouraged.

I began to tell him the wonderful ways people were helping us. I told him about the fund Mark Patredis and Jim Dunn had instigated at our church to help provide for us financially. I told him about Terry and Susan Potter adopting Jeremy and Tate as second sons and including them with their boys in almost everything they did. I told him about Loren Hall's lawn company mowing our yard, about Gary Pitcock giving me a gasoline credit card, about Mike Brooks taking Tate to ride horses.

He looked away as if taking it all in. Then he said, "I'm a lucky man."

Thinking I must have heard wrong, I said, "You're what?"

He took a deep breath and repeated, "I said I'm a lucky man."

I was shocked. "Steve, no one would look at you lying in this bed and think you were a lucky man."

"Then they would be looking in the wrong place," he said.

That attitude of gratitude only continued to grow and flourish as Steve continued to improve. He told me repeatedly that he was grateful to be alive, to watch his children grow, to be a part of their lives, even though he was so limited in what he could do with them.

Like most guys, Steve liked gadgets. His favorite gadget became his motorized wheelchair. Because he was not able to shift his weight, the chair was designed to shift it for him. We called it his "Lazyboy-on-Wheels." He could lean back in it like a recliner and lift his feet up so he could stretch out completely. He got very fast and could whiz all around our community in it.

While Steve already had remote control TV, we also found him a remote control radio. He used his remote control garage door opener to let himself in and out of the house. He would say to me, "This is a great time in history for the handicapped! Look at all the gadgets we have! Plus we get great parking." He said it partly in jest, but that was really how he felt. He was truly thankful for all the things that made his life a little easier.

One evening at a Bible study a friend said to Steve, "Steve, I've decided what your message is to the world. It's 'So, what's your excuse?'" How true. That was Steve's message and God's message: What's our excuse?

Is life hard? You bet it is! Do we all have circumstances beyond our control? Yes, most of us do. But God is in control, and he has asked us to give him thanks for that despite our circumstances. Does he need our thanks? I don't know—but we do. We need to give thanks, to cultivate the attitude of gratitude. It will be an anchor for our soul.

TWENTY

Letting Go

One afternoon when I was visiting with the psychologist at the hospital, I told her some of my struggles at home with my two boys and a new baby daughter. "I don't know how single parents do this all their life," I said.

Very gently she questioned: "And what if you had to?"

I was stunned by her frankness. Not that I hadn't asked myself the same question. I had just never allowed myself to dwell on it and had certainly never spoken it out loud.

"I guess if I had to," I replied slowly, searching my soul, "I would manage. I know God is able to help us through anything, but that's such a terrible thought I don't even want to think about it."

She didn't press me. Instead, she reached across the table and put her hand on my arm as she said, "Cyndi, many people can never imagine themselves making such an adjustment in their lives. But you cannot truly heal until you begin to conceive of a new kind of life. None of us know Steve's outcome at this point. But whatever it is, we do know it's going to create a different kind of life for you and your family. Accepting that fact is half the battle."

Kathleen planted a seed in me that day. In order for me to heal and lead the way for my children, I would have to be open to a new view of us. I would have to make a shift in my concept of who we were and what we looked like.

Loss forces us to think of ourselves in a new light. In order to be an anchor for our children, we may have to let go of the past.

It Takes Time

I did not want to let go of our old family picture and embrace a new one. The old one had been just fine, thank you. It had certainly not been perfect, but every day that Steve was gone from us, the old life looked better and better. Each time I opened the lens to a future without him, I recoiled.

Because Steve's prognosis was uncertain, for a long time I held on to my dream that one day life would return to normal. Even when I read or heard about the probabilities associated with Steve's condition, I didn't let it destroy my hope, because I knew God could do anything he chose to do with Steve's life. Slowly, over the weeks, months and years following the accident, I gave up my secret hopes a little at a time. Eventually the recovery Steve gained and the recovery I expected lined up. It was a lengthy process that God led me through.

Whether you're dealing with a serious injury or illness, a heartbreaking affair or a sudden death, give yourself time. We are most comfortable with the familiar. It takes awhile for new ideas to sink in. Don't force yourself, but allow God, as you are ready, to move you into a new arena.

Inventing a New Kind of Family

I would tell people, "If Steve had been the kind of dad who came home and read the paper, watched TV and went to bed, maybe we wouldn't miss him so much. But instead, he came home, played with the boys, gave them baths, read and sang to them at bedtime.

He rarely turned the TV on until they were asleep, unless it was a show we all were watching together." Steve's absence left a gaping hole in our family life that I especially noticed in the evenings and on the weekends.

I struggled with the idea of going to church without him, going to school programs alone or taking trips with just the kids and me. The experiences felt empty. Only with time did that feeling lessen. To be perfectly honest, it never went completely away for me, but it did get less intense. In those moments when I felt incomplete, I asked God to complete me. I asked him to be so close that I was aware of his constant companionship and his meeting of our needs.

The summer Katelyn was seven, she asked me to tell her some "Daddy stories." I began to relate some of the funniest memories we had of Steve. After telling her a couple of tales, she stopped me.

"I wish I had known my dad when he was like that."

"I wish you could have too, Katelyn. And I'm sorry you never got to." Then, thinking I could use this teachable moment, I added, "But you know, Katelyn, the Scriptures tell us that God will be a father to the fatherless. And I believe everything you missed in not having your dad, God will make up to you. I don't know how or when, I just believe he will. Just think of it, you have the God of the Universe as your father!"

"That sounds good," she remarked, "but he can't give me rides on his shoulders or come down here and play games with me."

She was right. There are certain things she missed growing up that she will never experience. There was something in her family life that was incomplete. But I continue to pray that God will make her complete in him, in his way and in his time. He will do this for all of us as we continue to invent a new kind of family.

When Deb's husband died, she told her older children their family life was like a book. "In that book are many chapters, and one of the most special chapters is our life with Dad. But now that Dad is gone, that chapter is done. We must turn the page and start a new chapter. We can choose not to make anything of the rest of our book, or we can look ahead to the new chapter and see what God has for us."

Feeling Illegitimate or Diminished

After Jackie's divorce, her two teenage girls told her, "We're not a real family." Jackie set them straight. "While we may not have a father in our home, *we are a real family.*" Like Jackie, we must remind our children and ourselves of this truth. Often.

Paula struggled when she had to move out of her four-bedroom home into an apartment. She remembered hearing fellow teachers at her school refer to problem kids as "apartment kids," and now hers belonged in that category.

When Ami's daughter Mary Rose started first grade after her father died, she told her mom, "Kids will make fun of me because I don't have a dad." Ami has no idea where that thought came from, but even at six years old, Mary was struggling with others' perception of her family as being different.

It helps to find other families who have gone through a similar experience. Sometimes this is just a matter of getting together with friends in your church or neighborhood. Other times, this need may be met in a more structured way.

Our children will take their cues from us. As we allow God to nurture our hurting hearts, he will help us let go of our idea of what a family *should* be and help us rebuild the one that *is.* It will not be the same family we had before, but it will be a home formed out of God's faithfulness and anchored in his goodness. It will be a home that can withstand the storms of life.

TWENTY-ONE

Redefine Yourself

After a family crisis, along with reinventing your family, you also have to redefine yourself. One reason death, divorce and major illness or injuries are so painful is that every part of our lives is affected. Also, we gain a large sense of our identity from our marriage and family life. When that is disrupted, so is our identity. One of the things we can do to be an anchor for our children is to cooperate with the Holy Spirit in redefining ourselves.

Like so many other things, this is a process. You may feel as if a large part of you is missing. There's a hole in your heart and life. Some people try to fill this hole in harmful ways: abusing alcohol or drugs, overworking, overspending or getting involved with someone else too quickly. Give yourself time to heal. As you do, God will give you a new vision of who you can be.

This did not come quickly for me. For many years, Steve's medical condition and the needs of my three children ordered my life. I once told a friend, "In some ways my life's purpose has changed very little. Before the accident I saw my role as Steve's helpmate—maintaining our home, partnering with him in ministry and occasionally helping with his work. After the wreck, I still saw myself primarily as Steve's helpmate—only now I was advocating for him at medical meetings, scheduling therapists and researching equipment for the handicapped."

After Steve died, those activities came to a screeching halt. It took some time just to reconfigure the picture of a life without him. The year after he died I had all three children in school. For the first time in eighteen years, I did not have a child at home during the day. I began to pray and think about what God might have for me.

I met with a couple of pastors' wives who had active speaking ministries to women and asked how I might get involved in my own speaking ministry. I called a former writing instructor to talk with her about some possibilities in writing. Cheri invited me to join a writing group she led that motivated and encouraged me. Opportunities began to open up for me both to speak and write.

When I started using my gifts and abilities, I found more healing and a new purpose to my life. I receive a tremendous sense of fulfillment as I share our family's story and explain how God kept us afloat. I've seen firsthand how God redeems our pain and uses it to help others.

God can give you, as well, a new picture of yourself and your family. It takes some work, but it's well worth the effort.

Rediscover Who You Are

Start by reevaluating who you are now. This is especially helpful if you married young. What are you passionate about? Look around you, do some reading, take a class. Find something you believe in. You may not have a lot of time right now, but you can begin to cultivate your interests.

After a painful divorce, your self-esteem may be very low. Don experienced this. "I felt like a throw-away," he says. "I thought no one would ever want me or love me again." If you have been the victim of abuse, this is especially true.

As you build a new life for yourself, take time to do things you enjoy that you can do now. Don't put aside everything until the kids are grown. Find ways to take care of yourself and learn what de-stresses you: hobbies, music, a massage, exercise, talking to a friend.

God can help you rebuild your self-worth as you process your grief and anger. As you take steps such as anchoring yourself in God, your self-worth will be affected. Again, a solid Christian counselor can also be of help.

Part of rediscovering who you are is savoring the things that bring you comfort or pleasure. Make a list of those things and keep it where you can easily refer to it. When you feel overwhelmed or that your emotions are getting out of control, check your list and find something to do that nurtures you. A few ideas:

- Relax in a bubble bath
- Read a book
- Take a walk
- Listen to music
- Work a puzzle
- Call a friend
- Go to a movie
- Sit on the porch with a cup of coffee

Debbie said that after her divorce she had trouble sleeping. she would get up in the middle of the night and work on jigsaw puzzles. It gave her mind something to focus on instead of her worry and fear. She also took bubble baths two or three times a week, locking out the world and her kids for a few minutes of solitude.

Make your own list. Find your fix and take time to do it.

Rethink Your Career

My friend Holly lost her husband in an airplane crash. She had developed an interest in photography before Tom's death, but once he was gone, it became an outlet for her, a place to pour her energy and creativity. She quickly became a much sought-after photographer in our area, known for her unique and artistic style. Holly would never say her business made up for her loss, but she would tell you it helped her redefine herself as a competent, creative woman with something to contribute.

Paula had been a teacher before her two girls were born. After her divorce, she had an outdated teaching certificate. She found a temporary job while she took the needed courses to update her degree. She then found a teaching job that proved to be a godsend. "For the hours I was at school, I completely forgot about my problems at home. I was totally absorbed in my work. It wasn't until I walked out of the building and headed to my car that it would all come back to me," she says. Teaching was a lifesaver for Paula, helping her earn a living and regain a life.

If you have been a stay-at-home mom, going back into the work force may be scary and overwhelming. There are resources now for women returning to work. Begin with a career counselor at your local junior college or vocational school. Take some tests to discover your aptitudes and abilities. Take advantage of organizations such as Displaced Homemakers. Even if you are forced to get a job immediately and it's not what you really want to do, continue to seek guidance and explore your options for the long run. Give this area to God. "Don't forget to tell him what you need and then thank him for his answers" (Phil 4:8).

Redirect Your Energy

Sometimes in order to open a new chapter of your life, you need to open yourself up to new ideas. Is there something you've always wanted to do? An interest you've always had in the back of your mind? A hobby you've wanted to pursue? Now may be the time. Take a painting class or a course in creative scrapbooking. Learn a new style of cooking or how to make jewelry. Do something as simple as getting a new hairstyle or getting a makeover at the local department store cosmetic counter. Don't be afraid to try something new as you reinvent yourself.

Remember to mend your body as well as your mind and soul. Stress takes a toll on us physically. Begin an exercise program. Walk your neighborhood, preferably with a friend. Join a gym. Take an aerobics class.

Help Someone Else

Debbie said the thing that made a personal difference for her in putting her life back together was deciding to tell others about her escape from an abusive marriage. "It was hard at first, but I found it very healing. It was wonderful to find that people still accepted me."

One of the ways God redeems our pain is to turn it around to help someone else. Paul writes, "Praise be to the God ... of all comfort, who comforts us in all our troubles, so that we can comfort those in any trouble with the comfort we ourselves have received from God" (2 Cor 1:3-4). No one can comfort us like another person who has been where we are—and who has come through the storm alive and well. When you become that person for someone, it helps him or her, but it also helps you to heal.

This may mean you invite a neighbor whose mate has been diagnosed with cancer over for coffee. You might offer to lead a divorce recovery group in your church. Look around for another single-parent family and ask them to join you for a picnic in the park. Volunteer. One of the best ways we help ourselves is by helping someone else.

You might want to symbolize the new life you are creating with an action—burying a hatchet or planting a garden. Whatever you decide to do, do it. As you redefine yourself, seeing yourself as a person of worth created in God's image, you will become an anchor for your children and a beacon of hope for others in their grief.

TWENTY-TWO

Develop an Eternal Perspective

T he door slammed with such force that I shuddered along with the walls.

"Mom," Tate cried, "where are you?"

Finding me, he poured out his trouble: "The big boys won't let me play basketball. I want you to go tell them they have to let me play!"

My seven-year-old had just returned from a neighbor's home. His older brother and his brother's friends were in the midst of a heated contest in our driveway.

"Wait until they finish this game," I told him, "then you can join in."

But Tate didn't want to wait. He followed me to the kitchen, still expecting me to intervene. When I persisted in doing nothing, he pleaded, "Aren't you going to do something? You own this house, you know. You own that basketball goal! *You could do something about this!*"

He was right. I did own the house and the goal, and I *could* do something about it. But I was choosing not to. At seven, Tate could not comprehend that. He saw me as indifferent at best, cruel at worst. Eventually he resigned himself to my decision and went outside to wait his turn.

I thought of my own conversation with God earlier in the day when I'd been vacuuming. I had dwelt on the circumstances of our life. After five months, Steve was finally beginning to emerge from his coma. How thrilled we were when we realized his long-term memory was intact, he could read our cards and he got the punch lines to our jokes. But there were still terrible physical problems, communication disorders and depression. He was recovering, but it was taking so long.

With each shove of the Hoover, I shot a thought to God. *You could do something about this, you know. You made Steve. You could fix him. I know he's getting better, but it's too slow. I'm tired of waiting. And I don't understand why a loving God won't do more.*

I recognized myself in Tate. Like my child, I knew who held the power to change the situation. And like him, I couldn't understand why he wouldn't act when and how I wanted.

As Tate's parent, I had a perspective he didn't have; I knew it was not ultimately in his best interests for me to intervene. But he couldn't understand what I knew.

Could it be that I was even less capable of understanding God's perspective than Tate was of mine? Could Steve's situation have some ultimate purpose that I could not fathom? I thought of Isaiah 55:8-9: "'For my thoughts are not your thoughts, neither are your ways my ways,' declares the Lord. 'As the heavens are higher than the earth, so are my ways higher than your ways and my thoughts your thoughts.'"

That day was a turning point for me. It didn't stop my pain or my questioning, but it helped me see that God knew and loved us in ways I might not comprehend; that he was in control, regardless of how it seemed; and that I could trust him with Steve's life as well as my children's and my own.

Developing an eternal perspective can make a difference in how we handle the small issues of life as well as the big ones. As with so many things, Steve had always been my best teacher of this lesson. When I would get frustrated with daily annoyances such as missing sneakers or spilled pop, Steve's blue eyes would twinkle at me and he'd say, "Oh, Lamb, lighten up! What's it going to matter one hundred years from now? Or ten? Or one?" It was his consistent way of reminding me not to take life too seriously and to remember that so much of our frustrations and even our real suffering are temporary. (When Steve's beloved Oklahoma Sooner football team lost to the University of Texas, I had my chance to remind him of our "one-hundred-year perspective." After all, I was originally from Texas!)

Steve's cultivation of that perspective before his accident helped him after life got really difficult. One morning I had feverishly gotten the boys off to school, rescued two-year-old Katelyn from snacking in the dog's bowl, spilled Steve's medication all over the counter and taken phone calls from a late nurse's aide when the doorbell rang. After accepting the delivery, I came back into the kitchen and found Steve sitting in his wheelchair crying. "What's the matter?" I cried, fearing he had hurt himself.

"Your life is so hard," he sputtered out, continuing to weep. "I'm so sorry this has happened to you."

I cried with him. "It is hard, honey. But your life is no picnic. I wouldn't want to change places with you."

He looked at me and said, "I wouldn't want to change places with you. I couldn't do what you do. I couldn't manage all this and the kids. I don't see how you do it."

I stopped what I was doing and bent down to him. "Steve, almost everything in your life has been taken away from you. You can't walk, you can't drive, you can't work and you can't even get to the bathroom by yourself. Don't tell me my life is hard. I don't see how you do it." I began to sob and he joined me.

For a while we stayed there, crying on each other's shoulders, sharing in our mutual grief over the life we had lost and the life we now had. We cried for ourselves and for each other. Then Steve said a remarkable thing: "I'm okay, Cyndi, really I am. If God can use this for his glory, then it's okay with me. After all," he reminded me, "it's all temporary. What's it going to matter one hundred years from now?" There it was again ... that "hundred-year perspective." If ever there was a time we needed it, now was the time.

Whatever it is that you and your family are dealing with—the death of a mate, an unwanted divorce, the loss of a dream—developing an eternal perspective can help you shoulder your grief. Your situation is not forever. God's Word tells us there are rewards for those who finish the race, despite the obstacles. You are not in this alone; God is with you for the long haul.

An eternal perspective anchors you amidst the deepest storms. It will hold you for years—not ten, not fifty, not a hundred.... Forever!

Epilogue

Our family sits between the ten-year anniversary of Steve's accident and the five-year anniversary of his death. Recently I spent the afternoon with my three children, now twenty, sixteen and ten. We set the time aside to commemorate Steve's accident. I had each child light a wick of a three-wick candle. I retold the story of their dad's accident and recovery. We looked through cards and letters and recounted the many ways God had taken care of us.

I reminded them of the redbud tree that we had ordered to be planted at Katelyn's newly built elementary school in their father's memory. We had dinner at one of Steve's favorite restaurants, Taco Bueno, before dropping by to visit the children's grandmother, Steve's mother. I also took them by Steve's grave before we returned home.

Our waters are calmer now, though not stagnant. Eighteen months ago I remarried. Mike is a widower who had lost his wife to cancer. He has three children, two of whom are married and one who is in college. Remarriage, even in the best of circumstances, brings its own turbulence, so once again my kids and I have all had to negotiate some rapids, although nothing like we've experienced before.

Mike and I reconnected when he moved to our city to join the staff at my church. We had known each other growing up in Dallas, but had not been close friends. That soon changed, and a year later we were married at the conclusion of one of our Sunday morning worship services.

Our pastor built the entire service around the faithfulness of God. The choir and orchestra performed the Brooklyn Tabernacle Choir piece, "He Is Faithful." Before the service, Mike and I had made videotapes of our individual testimonies of God's faithfulness to our families; these tapes were played at the conclusion of the sermon. Then the two of us, along with our children, joined the pastor on the platform as he led us through our vows. There was not a dry eye in the place.

We cried as a family and as a congregation as we remembered the suffering both our spouses had experienced. We wept in gladness that God had brought two broken people together, two people who understood grief and loss. We rejoiced at the possibilities that lay ahead.

Mike is my encourager and my biggest cheerleader. He believes in my gifts and prays the prayer of Jabez over me daily. He supports my weekend speaking trips. He loves my children and has willingly taken on a second family after having raised his own. He is attentive, affirming and hilarious. He is a prize!

Today Jeremy, my older son, is in college and engaged to be married to a wonderful girl. (Her parents have been my close friends since college days.) He will play his last season of college football next fall. Right now, Jer wants to teach and coach but remains open to wherever God wants to lead him and Laurie. He is mature beyond his years, with a wisdom and insight I believe were incubated in the crucible of suffering he entered into at age ten.

Tate is sixteen, class president, making a 3.7 grade point average—and he's the best-looking guy on his varsity baseball team. (I'm totally unbiased!) His deep bass voice and handsome physique are the package that houses an awesome heart. He's tender and sensitive, a great kid with a winsome smile. After the career he has planned in the major leagues and on the NASCAR circuit, he's not sure what God has for him.

Katelyn is energy wrapped in skin and topped with long blonde hair. Passionate about animals, she has five pets. She loves to read and write and draw and shop. Our fun is just beginning. She is bold and articulate, with a definite flair for the dramatic. God will use her courage one day. Until then, she can't wait to get to middle school.

All three kids got a healthy dose of their father's creativity, sense of humor and musical abilities. They make life fun and loud and very interesting. They are a blessing.

So far, everyone has stayed afloat. We've not made it completely to solid ground, but we are on our way. Chances are, we will hit perilous waters again, together or individually. My prayer is that with God's help, we will once again stay afloat.

I don't know what kind of turbulence you are facing today. But as you are navigating the children you love through rough waters, my prayer is that you will "grasp how wide and long and high and deep is the love of Christ" (Eph 3:18). It's bigger than any storm we might encounter. Hold on to the Father. He will not let you go!

Notes

Two
Be the Parent

1. Melinda Blau, *Families Apart: 10 Keys to Successful Co-Parenting* (New York: G.P. Putnam's Sons, 1993), 46, 98.

Three
Tell the Truth

1. M. Gary Neuman, *Helping Your Kids Cope With Divorce the Sandcastles Way* (New York: Time, 1998), 19.
2. Mary Ann Emswiler and James P. Emswiler, *Guiding Your Child Through Grief* (New York: Bantam, 2000), 245.
3. Edward Teyber, *Helping Children Cope With Divorce* (Don Mills, Ont.: Lexington, 1992), 38.

Four
Reassure Them

1. Emswiler and Emswiler, 29.
2. Neil Chetnik, *FatherLoss: How Sons of All Ages Come to Terms With the Deaths of Their Dads* (New York: Hyperion, 2001), 32.

3. Hanna McDonough and Christina Bartha, *Putting Children First: A Guide for Parents Breaking Up* (Toronto: Univ. of Toronto Press, 1999), 30.

Six
Listen Without Reacting

1. As quoted in Chetnik, 39.

Seven
Be Present

1. Teyber, 27.
2. Emswiler and Emswiler, 83.
3. McDonough and Bartha, 19.
4. Blau, 69.

Eight
Major on Majors

1. Carrie Lance, interviewed by Cyndi Lamb Curry on August 24, 2001.
2. Archibald Hart, *Helping Children Survive Divorce* (Dallas: Word, 1996), 55.
3. Vicki Lansky, *Divorce Book for Parents* (New York: New American Library, 1989), 30.

Nine
Keep Them Connected

1. Teyber, 116.
2. Florence Bienenfeld, *Helping Your Child Through Your Divorce* (Alameda, Calif.: Hunter House, 1995), 121.
3. Chetnik, 33.
4. Blau, 69.

Ten
Preserve Memories, Make New Traditions

1. Emswiler and Emswiler, 143-44.

Twelve
Get Help When You Need It

1. Emswiler and Emswiler, 164.
2. Emswiler and Emswiler, 165-69.
3. Doug Manning, *Lean On Me Gently: Helping the Grieving Child* (Oklahoma City: In-Sight Books, 1998), 27.

Thirteen
You Are Your Children's Anchor

1. Blau, 105.

Fifteen
Take Care of Yourself

1. Manning, 7.
2. Emswiler and Emswiler, 229.

Sixteen
Let Go of Anger and Resentment

1. Lansky, 31.
2. Hart, 34–35.
3. Hart, 44.
4. Blau, 74.

Bibliography

Bienenfeld, Florence. *Helping Your Child Through Your Divorce.* Alameda, Calif.: Hunter House, 1995.

Blau, Melinda. *Families Apart: 10 Keys to Successful Co-Parenting.* New York: G.P. Putnam's Sons, 1993.

Chetnik, Neil. *FatherLoss: How Sons of All Ages Come to Terms With the Deaths of Their Dads.* New York: Hyperion, 2001.

Edelman, Hope. *Motherless Daughters: A Legacy of Loss.* Boston: Addison-Wesley, 1994.

Emswiler, Mary Ann, and James P. Emswiler. *Guiding Your Child Through Grief.* New York: Bantam, 2000.

Hart, Archibald. *Helping Children Survive Divorce.* Dallas: Word, 1996.

Lansky, Vicki. *Divorce Book for Parents.* New York: New American Library, 1989.

Manning, Doug. *Lean On Me Gently: Helping the Grieving Child.* Oklahoma City: In-Sight, 1998.

McDonough, Hanna, and Christina Bartha. *Putting Children First: A Guide for Parents Breaking Up.* Toronto: Univ. of Toronto Press, 1999.

Neuman, M. Gary. *Helping Your Kids Cope With Divorce the Sandcastles Way.* New York: Time, 1998.

Teyber, Edward. *Helping Children Cope With Divorce.* Don Mills, Ont.: Lexington, 1992.

Wallerstein, Judith, Julia Lewis, and Sandy Blakeslee. *The Unexpected Legacy of Divorce: A 25 Year Landmark Study.* New York: Hyperion, 2000.

Wolfelt, Alan D. *Healing a Child's Grieving Heart: 100 Practical Ideas for Family, Friends, and Caregivers.* Fort Collins, Colo.: Companion Press, 2001.

——. *Healing a Teen's Grieving Heart: 100 Practical Ideas for Family, Friends, and Caregivers.* Fort Collins, Colo.: Companion Press, 2001.

Internet Sites

www.calmwaters.org. *Calm Waters*. A safe harbor for children whose lives have been changed by death or divorce.

www.centerforloss.com. *The Center for Loss and Life Transition.*

www.kidsplace.org. *The Kids' Place*. A center for grieving children and their families.

www.midlandcounty.org/foc/smile2.htm. *S.M.I.L.E.: Start Making It Livable for Everyone.*